Asian American Poetry

Asian American Poetry

THE NEXT GENERATION

Edited by

Victoria Chang

Foreword by Marilyn Chin

UNIVERSITY OF ILLINOIS PRESS

URBANA AND CHICAGO

© 2004 by the Board of Trustees
of the University of Illinois
All rights reserved
Manufactured in the United States
of America
1 2 3 4 5 C P 5 4 3 2 1
∞ This book is printed on
acid-free paper.

Library of Congress
Cataloging-in-Publication Data
Asian American poetry : the next
generation ; edited by Victoria M.
Chang ; foreword by Marilyn Chin.
p.   cm.
Includes bibliographical references
(p.   ) and index.
ISBN 0-252-02905-4 (cl. :
acid-free paper)
ISBN 0-252-07174-3 (pbk. :
acid-free paper)
1. American poetry—Asian American
authors. 2. Asian Americans—Poetry.
I. Chang, Victoria M. 1970–   .
PS591.A76 A83   2004
811'.6080895—dc22   2003019685

To my parents,

my sister,

and my husband, Todd

Contents

C. Dale Young

Foreword

MARILYN CHIN

At the cusp of the new millennium, we are looking for art that can best express our current human predicament: post-9/11, post–AIDS pandemic, post–Internet boom and bust, post–Generation X, post–Generation Why (Y), postfeminist, post–outside agitating era, post–crack and ecstasy, post–psychic numbing . . . The postmodern critics love to tell us over and over that there is no such thing as an authentic voice in late capitalism, that everything has been consumed and spent, that poetry workshops are sprouting all over the country like malls, and that the voices are indistinguishable from one another.

Meanwhile, a new patriotism springs out, and we tighten our borders. The twin towers of symbolic international prosperity have been blown into smithereens. A new American pride emerges from the ashes. We, from the margins, are expected to realign our allegiances and work with the majority. We are called to put down our ethnic pride and to fall into formation, front and center. To collect the "next generation" of Asian American poetry at this moment means both to assert our "specialness" as well as to showcase our spirit of cooperation and togetherness.

Perhaps it was easier for me, an immigrant poet—from what the editor of this anthology, Victoria M. Chang, calls the "first generation"—to ground my work in an old-fashioned minority discourse, fraught with the themes of racism, sexism, assimilation, and postcolonialism. I colored my poems with mega-Chinese-food tropes and deconstructed my cleaver-wielding grandmother with bliss. I was too young to be a sixties activist but old enough to feel the shadows of Vietnam, feminism, and the youth movement, filled with psychedelic hope and idealism—my generation forged an activist poetry, but with a refined craft we learned from master workshops. The fallow field was open for a new crop. If my generation had indeed laid "the groundwork," it would be the mission of the "next generation" to add a new layer of rich humus. It is our job as poets to write the poetry of "our times." This foreword is a means for me to pass the torch as a symbolic gesture. This anthology serves as part showcase, part call to arms. We must march onward, bear witness, and work with a conscious effort to build a magnificent, dynamic canon.

The introduction by Victoria M. Chang is rich with sociohistorical information and analysis and should be useful to students and poetry fans alike. The reader shall be pleased by the wide range of aesthetic proclivities and cross-fertilization. A variety of "schools" and sensibilities are represented—L=A=N=G=U=A=G=E poetry, East Coast neoformalism, West Coast hip, Whitmanesque sweeps, domestic quiet spaces, suburban landscapes, urban despair, love in angst and harmony, political rage. This anthology is a scintillating canvas with varying hues and emotions.

A Nick Carbó poem, such as "American Adobo," is written in a traditional lyric narrative, peopled and colored with the food and music of his neighborhood. Turn the pages and one will find Timothy Liu's "Assignation," written with a compressed, formal ear and erotic edge. These are recognizable traits by well-seasoned poets. There are equally pleasing pieces by surprising newcomers, voices and poets with whom I've yet to be acquainted. The Vietnam-born Mông-Lan's poems are a cross-fertilization of East and West, of motherland and new soil. Some of her stanzas are like gestural paintings, where the lines float delicately as Buddha's lotus pads. The fine phrasing works hand in hand with the compelling visuals, giving the white page a quiet, distilled, transcendent beauty. This is a true bicultural imagination brewing. Then there are the postmodern elliptical fragments of Adrienne Su and Cathy Park Hong, who use the page as a compositional field, but unlike Mông-Lan's delicate lines, theirs refuse a beautiful classical flow, aiming instead for jarring interruptions and daring juxtapositions, mimetic of our fragmented identities in a complex age of overloaded synapses and short attention spans.

Perhaps the most compelling aspect of this collection is that it pays respectful homage to other Asian American anthologies and poets before this era, with a strong conviction that Asian American poetry is more than only a blip or aberration on the literary lineage. Our poetry is not a static enterprise but a thriving, historical progression. Our identities are multitudinous, multilayered, and polyphonic. Obviously, after several generations of influential anthologies, we are no longer sojourners with a provisional visa, we are citizens of this culture, and we are here to stay.

Introduction

VICTORIA M. CHANG

This could not be a more exciting time for Asian American poetry. In the 1980s and 1990s, an increasing number of Asian American poets, including Ai, Cathy Song, John Yau, Li-Young Lee, Marilyn Chin, and Garrett Hongo, were featured in literary journals, won awards, and published books. They were the first generation[1] of Asian American poets to receive widespread recognition in the American literary community. Building on this legacy and often striking off in new directions, a new generation of Asian American poets has come of age. *Asian American Poetry: The Next Generation* presents the best of this recent work, laying the groundwork for readers as well as broadening the scope of American literature.[2]

While the accomplishments of these first-generation poets are significant milestones, the history of Asian American poetry extends back more than a century. In the 1890s, Sadakichi Hartmann published some of the first symbolist poetry in English. Yone Noguchi published imagist poetry during this time as well. During the first decades of the twentieth century, H. T. Tsiang published Marxist-internationalist poetry. In the 1940s, Toyo Suyemoto wrote rhymed quatrains in internment camp journals, while Jose Garcia Villa and Carlos Bulosan wrote religious and proletarian poetry, respectively. In the 1960s, poets such as Fred Wah, Joy Kagawa, Zulfikar Ghose, Jessica Hagedorn, and Lawson Inada began to publish their poems, and a decade later the feminist poets Mitsuye Yamada and Janice Mirikitani published their first volumes, *Camp Notes and Other Poems* (1976) and *Awake in the River* (1978), respectively. The 1970s produced a string of anthologies of Asian American prose and poetry, such as *Aiiieeeee! An Anthology of Asian American Writings* (1974) and *Asian American Heritage: An Anthology of Prose and Poetry* (1974).[3] These Asian American poets set the stage for the first-generation Asian American poets and those that followed.

The poetry of what I refer to as the "first generation" tended to focus on issues of culture, identity, family, politics, ethnicity, and place. These poets generally wrote "protest literature," exposing their inferior treatment by the mainstream culture. Li-Young Lee's poem "Persimmons" presents some of the complex issues that many Asian American poets in the past addressed. Lee uses the complexities of language and the difficulties of translating, both linguistically and culturally, to portray the cultural duality of his childhood. In the poem, persimmons symbolize his cultural differences from mainstream society and his relationship with his blind, elderly father. In one section, the poem shows Lee's teacher punishing him for not understanding the difference between "persimmon" and "precision":

In sixth grade Mrs. Walker
slapped the back of my head
and made me stand in the corner
for not knowing the difference
between *persimmon* and precision.
How to choose

persimmons. This is precision. . . .
Other words
that got me into trouble were
fight and *fright, wren* and *yarn.*
Fight was what I did when I was frightened,
fright was what I felt when I was fighting.
Wrens are small, plain birds,
yarn is what one knits with.
Wrens are soft as yarn.
My mother made birds out of yarn.
I loved to watch her tie the stuff;
a bird, a rabbit, a wee man. . . .[4]

Marilyn Chin's "How I Got That Name" discusses the common challenges of assimilation that confronted Asian immigrants. Her speaker voices complex feelings about preserving culture and assimilation. She accepts and perhaps even cherishes her family's past but understands that she also must assimilate into American culture. She points to a feeling common among Asian Americans at that time: a feeling of being a lost race, neither "black nor white / neither cherished nor vanquished":

I am Marilyn Mei Ling Chin
Oh, how I love the resoluteness
of that first person singular
followed by that stalwart indicative
of "be," without the uncertain i-n-g
of "becoming." Of course,
the name had been changed
somewhere between Angel Island and the sea,
when my father the paperson
in the late 1950s
obsessed with a bombshell blond
transliterated "Mei Ling" to "Marilyn."
And nobody dared question
his initial impulse—for we all know
lust drove men to greatness,
not goodness, not decency. . . .

So here lies Marilyn Mei Ling Chin,
married once, twice to so-and-so, a Lee and a Wong,
granddaughter of Jack "the patriarch"
and the brooding Suilin Fong,
daughter of the virtuous Yuet Kuen Wong
and G. G. Chin the infamous,
sister of a dozen, cousin of a million,
survived by everybody and forgotten by all.
She was neither black nor white,
neither cherished nor vanquished,
just another squatter in her own bamboo grove
minding her poetry—.[5]

Lee and Chin's work, as well as that of other first-generation Asian American poets, resonated with poets and readers in the past and continues to move and challenge readers today. However, the current poetic landscape is flourishing with new Asian American poets, forty years of age and younger, such as Timothy Liu, Marisa de los Santos, Cathy Park Hong, Rick Barot, C. Dale Young, Mông-Lan, and Vandana Khanna. Some among this new generation continue to write in styles or about topics similar to their predecessors, while many more are expanding the boundaries of Asian American poetry and breaking conventional patterns with new subject matter, fresh language, and powerful voices. Regardless of subject matter, style (by which I mean many craft elements such as language, the line and white space, the stanza, rhyme, form, and syntax) or voice, however, there is a thread that ties these next-generation poets together: they are part of a thriving community that is different from that of a generation ago. They are bolder about sexual topics and other previously taboo subjects, and they write less about ethnic or political issues. Their themes are more mainstream American, dealing with gay and lesbian lifestyles, voyeurism, and gender. They also write in innovative styles (experimenting with the line, white space, and stanza) and new voices.

In terms of subject matter, some next-generation poets carry on traditional concerns by writing "coming of age literature" or poems about parent-child relationships, rebellion, feelings of being uniquely misunderstood, bewilderment, and vulnerability in the face of the adult world. Such universal topics span generations. Brian Komei Dempster and Lee Ann Roripaugh, for example, write about Japanese internment camps, as did James Masao Mitsui and others from the prior generation. Adrienne Su writes about family and culture in poems such as "Savannah Crabs," as does Tina Chang in "Journal of the Diabetic Father":

II.

My mother wears paper roses in her wig.
Winter, in the kitchen, mice eat their way
through air to reach a nest of bananas.

There is nothing to do but let them go.
She tells me to talk to no one.
I talk to no one. Once I reach the roof

I read a Cantonese mystery.
The children below run,
breaking the windows with sticks.

III.

They call my father King of Burned Pots
as he stands before columns of dishes
in the back of the restaurant,

his arms immersed in brown water,
pork grease and mussel shells.
Hidden behind a veil of white steam

he is washing, always washing.
And I imagine the width
his tired shoulders.

Themes of exile, alienation, and difference are other traditional subjects of Asian American poetry. For instance, the collection *Leaving Yuba City* by the first-generation poet Chitra Banerjee Divakaruni focuses on the South Asian immigrant experience. She writes about her childhood in Darjeeling, a district in the state of West Bengal in India, as well as about the lives of persecuted Punjab farmers who immigrated to Yuba City, California.[6] Following in the footsteps of Divakaruni, Chin, and numerous others, some next-generation poets set poems in countries different from where they were born or where their heritage lies. Examples include Pimone Triplett writing about Thailand, Vandanna Khanna writing about India, and Mông-Lan writing about Vietnam in her poem "Field":

Crows land like horses' neighs
rush of rocks

how many buffaloes
does it take to plow a disaster?
how many women to clean
up the mess?

shoots of incense
hotly in her hands
she bows towards the tombstones
face of her son
how many revolutions for us to realize?

her windless grey hair
becomes her   she knows this
there is no reason
to dye what she's earned

rain quiet as wings

on her back

Despite such similarities in subject matter, there are extensive examples of next-generation Asian American poets venturing into new subject matter. For example, Timothy Liu, C. Dale Young, and Rick Barot write freely and openly about their relationships with men. Many of Liu's poems (notably in his most recent book, *Hard Evidence*) are honest and vivid in their eroticism. He often combines sexual and serene images. For example, in his poem "Winter," "A school of swollen tongues darting at his balls" is followed immediately by, "Frozen waterfalls embroidered into silk." Although eroticism is not the primary focus of his work, Barot explores his lover's physical qualities in "Occupations":

Astronomer to the ten Turkish moons
counted out on your fingernails.

Surveyor to the shiny silicate scar
of the childhood cut on your brow.

Geologist to the fault-line crack
your wrist has long since healed from.

Treasurer to the coin of vaccination
darkly minted on your left arm.

Farmer to the stubbled acreage
of your chin, to the nocturnal root.

In a similar vein, Lisa Asagi writes about her desires for women in "Soundtrack for Home Movie No. 3," while Aimee Nezhukumatathil describes a male lover in sensual rich language in "Mouth Stories": "The skin between your shoulder / and neck is fresh on my tongue." In her poem "Panopticon," Brenda Shaughnessy talks about vibrators and voyeurism. Rick Noguchi's series of poems develops an unusual story about a surfer named Kenji Takezo, whose passion for the ocean resonates from the pages.

In addition to subject matter, the next-generation poets also use style to make connections with and to distinguish their work from that of earlier poets. Some new Asian American poets continue to write in more traditional ways, in a style one critic has described as "a distillation of some of those things that have made memoirs by Asian and Asian American women phenomenally popular: associative, personal, intimate, emotive."[7] Poets such as Marisa de los Santos and C. Dale Young evoke a traditional feel by writing in even stanzas. Rick Barot's stanzas are symmetrical. Brian Komei's work is more traditionally narrative, and Adrienne Su also writes in a narrative style, while using form in deft and interesting ways through slant rhyme (near rhyme), as in the last words of each line in "Savannah Crabs":

Bluish and thirsty, packed tight as oranges,
they come from the coast in the iced trunk
of the blue Buick our aunt drives. She's sunk
in thoughts of dinner and not the tinges

of dread that will stain her African violets
as she tends a back pain. She does not think
of her mother, who'll die this fall under pink
bedclothes without a goodnight; the eyelets

of her gown will spell the Chinese words
for *loneliness, lovelessness, white birds.*

In contrast, some of the new-generation poets use style as a domain for innovation, experimenting with language, the line and white space, the stanza, rhyme, form, and syntax (the structure of words, phrases, clauses, and sentences). There are a number of prose poems, such as Oliver de la Paz's series, Lisa Asagi's poems, Cathy Park Hong's "Not Henry Miller but Mother," Warren Liu's "Be You Ever So Lonesome," and Jon Pineda's "Birthmark." The new writing is often sparse, with less of a storytelling style. In "The Pink House in Four Variations," Brian Komei Dempster tells a story about rape using tight, brief images:

We are steaks on a board, freezing the son's blade.
Our mouths his well filling with dirt and piss. Grass,
bugs fucking upside down. Between our teeth, his cock
riveting. The throat shreds the heart into songbirds.

Brenda Shaughnessy's diction is fresh and original. To use her own words, she "'picks apart English'" and "'beat[s] it up a little.'"[8] Her work is brassy, erotic, and inventive. In the first poem in her book *Interior with Sudden Joy,* Shaughnessy uncovers unusual English words such as "serviceberries" (the shadbush or one of its fruit) and "gloxinia" (any of several tropical South American plants of the genus Sinningia). Shaughnessy's poem "Interior with Sudden Joy" exhibits her innovative playfulness with language:

To come into my room is to strike strange.
My plum velvet pillow & my hussy spot
the only furniture.

Red stripes around my ankles, tight
as sisters. We are maybe fourteen, priceless
with gooseflesh.

Our melon bellies, our mouths of tar. Us four:
my mud legged sister, my bunched-up self,
the dog & the whirligig just a prick on the eye.

We are all sewn in together, but the door is open.
The book is open too. You must write in red
like Jesus and his friends.

Although more narrative and lyrical in nature, Oliver de la Paz's collection of poems about a Filipino boy who yearns to fly is mesmerizing and inventive in its prose form. A good example is "When Fidelito Is the New Boy at School":

He is a frequent eclipse . . . a shadow on fire. The light breaks over the schoolyard and a hallucination of evenly cropped trees in stride moves the glass. As the dusk forms of spruce pass his face, he disappears.

He keeps his mouth shut and his palms open despite the steady drum of spit-wads, kid-song, and the long clock's nervous face. Bells refuse to breathe. And the wide hours wait for doors to open.

Fidelito gazes outside. There are other milder distractions: some of the children eat their shirts and some burst into rain. A road burns into a corner. In the power lines above the playground, a grackle's steel eye murders the earth. And the sky, now perfect for flight, is open like the older mouth of our moon.

Many of the next-generation poets, such as Jennifer Chang, Cathy Park Hong, Mông-Lan, and Warren Liu, experiment with the stanza, white space, and syntax in exciting and innovative ways. Warren Liu experiments with double lines and Adrienne Su with single lines, with fragments, phrases, and images for stanzas. Mông-Lan indents her poems and leaves white space within lines. She often interrupts her lines with white space instead of using traditional punctuation such as commas or periods. She also alters syntax by leaving out verbs. This can be seen in her poem "Ravine":

> the back of your neck
>   is a bird's shadow ascending
> your spine a line
>   a ravine where things are lost:
> marbles   the sound of a cello
> faded photos   brittle letters
>   I lace your body with my hands
>   your legs   loaves of bread
>   your feet   slippery fish
>   broken fins
> swimming through uncharted waters

Beyond subject matter and style, some next-generation poets write poetry that resembles the quieter, subtler, and more pensive voices of past Asian American poets such as Li-Young Lee. A language of quiet grace marks Marisa de los Santos's work, and Pimone Triplett's work is also graceful. Likewise, C. Dale Young asks questions in a meditative manner, as in his poem "Moonlight Cocktail":

. . . .

Lying at the foot of the bed last night reading,
you were half-naked but clothed in bright light.
Despite all the years, I still study you.

Outside the bar, just over your shoulder,
the city sits under a darkening sky
and a new moon is making an appearance—
even now, we talk about the moon.

In contrast, many next-generation poets, such as Cathy Park Hong, Paisley Rekdal, Monica Youn, and Suji Kwok Kim, have a distinctly modern edginess and attitude within their language, with a certain air of feminine strength. For example, in her poem "All the Aphrodisiacs," Hong unabashedly explores traditionally unfeminine words such as "cock":

What are the objects that turn me on: words—

han-gul: the language first used by female entertainers, poets,
        prostitutes.

The sight of shoes around telephone wires, pulleyed by their laces, the blunt word cock.

Similarly, in terms of voice, Rekdal's work has a sauciness rarely found in works by women in the past, as in her poem "Anniversary Song":

Look at us there on the museum steps, giggling before the Asian
stone camels and God! The strangers my mother invited to our
        reception

In photographs spit bubbles out of yellow plastic hoops,
soap suds dive bombing our knee-length chiffons.

If I'd known then what I don't give a hoot about now—
that even the bridesmaids might have preferred to hurl

invectives or Silly Putty at the guests than blush kisses
against our relatives' damp cheeks, that half the drunken

wedding party would later threaten to kill themselves or divorce—
perhaps we wouldn't have allowed ourselves

to be paraded this way. Who were we to be so happy
among our depressed, gay, single friends?

In summary, Asian American poets from the past generation have in-
fluenced this new generation. However, the new generation experiments
with various aspects of subject, style, and voice. This experimentation and
innovation suggests that these next-generation Asian American poets are
marking a physical separation from the past generation, casting off out-
moded styles and subjects and moving forward without boundaries.

A brief exploration of the roots of these differences is warranted. They
primarily stem from societal and demographic shifts. The next-generation
poets are mostly from Generation X—they were born between 1961 and
1981, and they mostly grew up with no one at home after school, a self-
reliant, skeptical, perplexed, politically inactive, searching, and vegged-out
population. They watched the debut of MTV and the Challenger explo-
sion. They are different from Baby Boomers, who have a strong set of ide-
als and traditions and are generally more family-oriented, fearful of the
future, politically conservative and active, and moderately socially liberal.

The new subject matter, styles, and voices of Asian American poets stem
also from ethnic shifts in American society. Over the last several decades,
Asian Americans have become more diverse. In the year 2000, the U.S.
Census Bureau, for the first time in history, gave Americans the option to
"check all that apply" in terms of ethnicity. Of the total population of 281
million Americans, 6.8 million people, or 2.4 percent, reported more than
one race. Of the 10 million Asian Americans, 2 percent reported that they
were Asian as well as one or more other races.[9] By 1998, the number of
interracial marriages in the United States had grown from 149,000 in 1960
to more than 1.3 million. The number of Asian American interracial mar-
riages in the United States has also increased, however data in this area
remains slim. The Census Bureau states that from 1960 to 1980, the num-
ber of Asian/Pacific Islander marriages with a Caucasian increased from
47,000 to 180,000. Data beyond that point are difficult to obtain, but Lar-
ry Hajime Shinagawa, an assistant professor at Sonoma State University,
asserts that by 1990, Asian interracial marriages surpassed one million (this
number is likely inflated, given the 1.3 million interracial marriages in gen-
eral by 1998).[10]

One indication of the growing diversity of Asian Americans, and per-
haps of their more fluid sense of ethnic boundaries, is that it has become

more challenging to identify Asian American poets by their surnames alone.[11] Examples include Brenda Shaughnessy, Pimone Triplett, Lee Ann Roripaugh, Brian Komei Dempster, Paisley Rekdal, Monica Ferrell, and C. Dale Young. What percentage of Asian ethnicity qualifies a poet as Asian American? Brenda Shaughnessy is half-Japanese and half-Irish American; Pimone Triplett is half-Thai, half-European American; Lee Ann Roripaugh is half-Japanese, half-European American; Jon Pineda is half-Filipino, half-European American; Brian Komei Dempster is half-Japanese, half-European American; Paisley Rekdal is half-Chinese, half-Norwegian; Monica Ferrell is half-Caucasian and half-South Asian; and C. Dale Young is a quarter Asian ($^1/_8$ East Indian and $^1/_8$ Chinese), half-Caucasian, and a quarter Latino. Self-identification has become the rule, rather than any arbitrary designation of a minimum percentage.

Another indication of the growing diversity of Asian Americans is the shift in the ethnic makeup of poets featured in Asian American poetry anthologies in the past versus that of poets featured in *Asian American Poetry: The Next Generation*. For example, in *The Open Boat*, published in 1993, among the thirty-one featured poets, 32 percent are Chinese American (born in the United States), 23 percent are Japanese American (born in the United States), 13 percent are Chinese American (born in Asia), 10 percent are multiethnic, 10 percent are South Asian (born in South Asia), 7 percent are Filipino American (born in the Philippines), 3 percent are Japanese American (born in Japan), and 3 percent are Filipino American (born in the United States).[12]

A decade later, *Asian American Poetry: The Next Generation* demonstrates a dramatic increase in multiethnic poets and an increase in Korean American, Vietnamese American, Thai American, and Filipino American poets. We see decreases in Chinese and Japanese American poets and a mild decrease in South Asian American poets. This anthology breaks down as follows: 32 percent multiethnic, 18 percent Chinese American (born in the United States), 14 percent Filipino American (born in the Philippines), 11 percent Korean American (born in the United States), 7 percent Japanese American (born in the United States), 4 percent Filipino American (born in the United States), 4 percent South Asian (born in the United States), 4 percent South Asian (born in South Asia), and 2 percent Vietnamese American (born in Vietnam). Also, many more of the next-generation poets were born in the United States or had spent a significantly greater amount of time in the United States compared with the prior generation. Thus the differences in subject, style, and voice are due to obvious generational differences but also to an increasing diversity of Asian Americans.

*

Secondly, beyond presenting innovative explorations in subject matter, style, and voice, this anthology is also a response to an increasing interest in Asian American studies and specifically in Asian American poetry. This can be attributed to the mushrooming of the Asian American population in recent decades. According to the U.S. Census Bureau, in 1990 there were 6.9 million Asian and Pacific Islanders in the United States, or 2.8 percent of the population. That number had increased to over 10 million and 4 percent of the population by 2001.[13] The number of Asians increased faster than the total population of the United States, which grew by 13 percent from 249 million in 1990 to 281 million in 2000. In addition, according to the *New York Times,* by 1999 there were more than forty-three Asian American studies programs at universities across the country—twice as many as a decade earlier.[14] As Asian Americans become more of a presence in the United States, their voices and experiences become more influential in a variety of arenas, including literature and the academy.

*

Finally, *Asian American Poetry: The Next Generation* takes its place beside the growth of anthologies that cater to specific subgroups of readers, a development that indicates readers' strong desire for editorial expertise. Alongside the omnipresent general anthologies such as the *Norton Anthology of English Literature,* recent specialized anthologies such as *The New Young American Poets,* edited by Kevin Prufer, and *American Poetry: The Next Generation,* edited by Gerald Costanzo and Jim Daniels, reflect chronological and demographic markers such as the new millennium, the aging of the Baby Boomers, and the maturation of Generation X.[15] These anthologies reflect the desire of editors and readers to differentiate new poets from their predecessors.

In addition to generation-specific anthologies, a number of Asian American poetry and poetry/prose anthologies have been published in recent decades, ranging from the watershed *Aiiieeeee!* to *The Forbidden Stitch: An Asian American Women's Anthology,* edited by Shirley Geok-lin Lim and Mayumi Tsutukawa. However, no anthology has specifically showcased the work of the new generation of Asian American poets. Even Walter K. Lew's *Premonitions: The Kaya Anthology of New Asian North American Poetry,* while an interesting and a lively addition to American literature, focuses on experimental poetry and features only previously unpublished work.[16]

*

The editorial aim of *Asian American Poetry: The Next Generation* was to gather the best work of the new Asian American poets, including traditional and experimental poets. Suggestions for poets potentially to include came from literary journals, books, other anthologies, poets, editors, and academics across the country. Poets under consideration provided additional suggestions, and the list of names grew rapidly. Uppermost among selection criteria was the quality of work itself rather than the goal of achieving a balanced representation of various ethnicities, gender, or other personal characteristics. More than 150 poets from across the country, writing in a wide range of styles and about all kinds of topics, sent in poetry manuscripts for consideration. Some had published books, while many had not.[17] A few were still undergraduates; others were MFA students or had attained MFA degrees. Each poet submitted at least twenty pages of poetry, preferably an entire manuscript in progress. Poets that had published books submitted newer work for consideration. Unpublished and previously published poems were considered.

The twenty-eight poets and nearly two hundred pages of poetry gathered here are notable for their ambition in subject matter, style, and voice. These poems avoid cliché and use fresh, innovative language to express universal human emotions as well as ethnically distinctive experiences and perceptions. Poems that mimic the subjects and images of the first generation (such as poems that deconstruct "cleaver-wielding grandmother[s]," in Marilyn Chin's words) without reaching for new heights and challenging previous boundaries were ultimately not selected. But newness was not valued simply for the sake of newness. The same rigor was applied to "experimental" poetry as traditional poetry.

It was not long ago that the editors of *The Forbidden Stitch* declined to publish manuscripts that used experimental forms and lacked a "recognizable Asian voice." *Asian American Poetry: The Next Generation* reflects a shift away from this ideal of a "recognizable Asian voice" and toward poetry that transcends racial, gender, and cultural boundaries. Garrett Hongo was correct in celebrating the literary achievements of Asian Americans in 1993. By celebrating such achievements, he was not depoliticizing Asian Americans, like some literary critics contend.[18] Does it always have to be so black and white—the bitter and angry political activists who take pride in protesting their inferior treatment by the mainstream culture versus the "whitewashed" mainstream sell-outs who aim to succeed within the greater literary community, or like Hongo, aim to showcase the widespread recognition of Asian American poets? There will always be those who do not believe we have made enough progress in the literary community and still others who believe our generation has made too much "progress" assimilating—that this new generation of Asian American poets is just the depressing result of assimilation, a generation that seems to have forgotten about its cultural ties and one that prides itself on differences from the previous generation of Asian American poets.

The exciting innovations in Asian American poetic art in terms of subject matter, style, and voice combined with the increased interest in Asian American poetry and anthologies in general constitute advancement, improvement, and evolution. The change is literary evolution and, even greater, human evolution—the good kind—the kind to celebrate, particularly amidst the events of September 11, 2001, and all of the other "de-evolution" of our violent times. These new Asian American poets have captured the power of the past but have ventured into new territories and discovered, created, and revealed new voices and styles. *Asian American Poetry: The Next Generation* showcases this new work without losing the past and avoids demarcating separations between "mainstream" and more "alternative" Asian American poets. We ask you to let these poems speak for themselves.

Notes

1. "First generation" does not imply that no other Asian American poets existed before; I use the term to refer to those that achieved widespread literary recognition.
2. I struggled with the decision of what to title the anthology: "Asian American Poetry: The Next Generation" versus "Asian Pacific American Poetry: The Next Generation" or "Asian and Pacific Islander American Poetry: The Next Generation." I understand the significance and importance of inclusion of and respect for the Pacific Islander community, but I ultimately decided upon the simpler, cleaner, and less cumbersome *Asian American Poetry: The Next Generation.* I am aware that some may view the title as a "step back"; however, I hope that those individuals or groups might see beyond the title and appreciate the greater vision and purpose of the anthology.
3. Mitsuye Yamada, *Camp Notes and Other Poems* (New York: Kitchen Table/Women of Color Press, 1976); Janice Mirikitani, *Awake in the River* (San Francisco: Isthmus Press, 1978); *Aiieeeee! An Anthology of Asian American Writings,* ed. Frank Chin et al. (Garden City, N.Y.: Doubleday, 1974); *Asian American Heritage: An Anthology of Prose and Poetry,* ed. David Hsin-Fu Wand (New York: Pocket Books, 1974). The sym-

bolist movement emphasized nonstructured "internalized" poetry that, for lack of better words, describes thoughts and feelings in disconnected ways and places logic, formal structure, and descriptive reality in the back seat. Their models were Charles Baudelaire and Walt Whitman; the symbolists in turn influenced twentieth-century modernist poets such as Ezra Pound, T. S. Eliot, and the surrealists. Yonejiro (Yone) Noguchi (1875–1947) was the first Japanese national to publish poetry in English. He was born near Nagoya in 1875 and traveled to the United States in 1893. He soon established a reputation among the imagist poets of San Francisco. See Juliana Chang, "Reading Asian American Poetry," *MELUS* 21:1 (Spring 1996): 81.

4. Li-Young Lee, "Persimmons," in *The Rose* (New York: BOA Editions, 1986), 17.

5. Marilyn Chin, "How I Got That Name," in *Phoenix Gone, the Terrace Empty* (Minneapolis: Milkweed Press, 1994), 16.

6. Chitra Banerjee Divakaruni, *Leaving Yuba City* (New York: Anchor, 1997).

7. Gary Gach, "Sheer Poetry," *AsianWeek* 14 (February 19, 1993): 26.

8. Qtd. in "Writers on the Verge," *Village Voice Literary Supplement,* April–May 1999.

9. Because this is the first time the U.S. Census Bureau collected such data, there are no prior data to compare these statistics to. However, most agree that the number of ethnically mixed Americans is significantly higher than in the past.

10. Stacy Lavilla, "The Minority Interracial Couples," *AsianWeek,* 19 (April 9–15, 1998): 12. In addition, 36 percent of young Asian Pacific American men born in the United States married white women, and 45 percent of U.S.-born Asian Pacific American women married white husbands.

11. This brings up an interesting issue, as Asian Americans lose their "tags," or their surnames that clearly identify them as Asian American. Does it make it easier or harder for them to publish their work, or is this irrelevant? It seems like it would be easier, since they would be considered in the pool of all other poets. But this assumes that ethnicity doesn't matter. In fact, some editors might be more apt to publish an author with an apparently Asian surname with diversity in mind. This is a question with no concrete answer, but an interesting one, nonetheless.

12. *The Open Boat,* ed. Garrett Hongo (New York: Anchor, 1993).

13. U.S. Census Bureau <http://www.census.gov>.

14. Somini Sengupta, "Asian American Programs Are Flourishing at Colleges," *New York Times,* June 9, 1999.

15. *The New Young American Poets,* ed. Kevin Prufer (Carbondale: Southern Illinois University Press, 2000); *American Poetry: The Next Generation,* ed. Gerald Costanzo and Jim Daniels (Pittsburgh: Carnegie Mellon University Press, 2000).

16. *The Forbidden Stitch: An Asian American Women's Anthology,* ed. Shirley Geok-lin Lim and Mayumi Tsutukawa (Corvalis, Oreg.: Calyx Books, 1988), 13; *Premonitions: The Kaya Anthology of New Asian North American Poetry,* ed. Walter K. Lew (New York: Kaya Press, 1995).

17. Note that several poets had their first books picked up for publication after being included in this anthology (publication was certainly not a prerequisite).

18. Victor Bascara, "Hitting Critical Mass," *Hitting Critical Mass: A Journal of Asian American Cultural Criticism* 1:1 (Fall 1993), online at <http://socrates.berkeley.edu/~critmass/v1n1/bascaraprint.html>.

Asian American Poetry

April 14

On the second floor of my sister's house. Lying down on the carpet of a room, surrounded by toys. Between two child beds. One shaped like a car. On the short white dresser, a small ball of water in which an orange plastic fish bobs mechanically in circles. And I wish it could stop. And I am wondering if there is really a thing called stop. How it seems to have grown into an impossible thing. The motions of this living. The way the air is unable to be still even in this room. I can feel it moving over the cells of skin on my feet and my face. Not able to sleep but so tired. As the house is being moved into one more day.

April 15

Strange sounds are coming through the plumbing of the house. There are canals and streams in the walls. Invisible systems even for water. Hidden in the clean white angles and sturdy carpet the color of sand. I am standing in the hallway about to turn off the last light. Before going to sleep. I have seven nights left. Seven more times I can do this. And from this thought appears a small green radar screen. Illuminating like a clock with only one arm. There are no numbers. An endless and even pulse. Sweeping around and around my chest.

April 22

Stepping out of the front door, into the middle of the cul de sac, how it has nothing to do with the sky but the positioning of everything and everyone sleeping and unable to sleep beneath it. And for the first time I feel like I do not have to leave tomorrow. Inside this thought is a yellow, an orange feeling. Twenty four hours from now I could be twenty five hundred miles away. Unpacking, going through piles of mail. Or I could be asleep in a house or apartment not far away. Having never ever left, at rest in another pattern for daylight. And here I am. A car driving by slows down to see what I am doing outside so late and drives on. I tell it I don't know. I don't know where I am going anymore. But something is happening. Maybe it is the wind. Maybe it is a lack of sleep. But it feels like one by one ropes are being untied and tossed onto a boat I am standing on. It is rocking. It is slowly sinking. And tonight it feels like I am getting ready to swim for a very long time.

Soundtrack for Home Movie No. 3

We are on a train moving through January in Japan. Light
is gathering outside the window.

So much snow.

Miles of brightness.

We sit in the first seats of the front car and watch
the conductor motion, with right gloved hand. To something
or someone not in our field of vision.

As if making a room for what is occurring.

We are so far away

We are a thin crimson line being drawn on a map.
You look at your boots. When the train turns
there is nothing. Only a river.

Here a small ellipse of earthly water.
Sulfur thick and lava hot. Surrounded by frost under a sky
swept clean. By lateness.

You are upstairs, asleep in the inn.
Between comforters light and warm like hair.

You are here on a long and complicated business trip.
I am here because I am the daughter you think
has a sense of direction.

This does not mean I do not know how to get lost.

I am the only one here. In this isolated moment
which could be easily mistaken.

A skier from a city not far from here asks,
"Why are you not married yet?"
When she stands, I follow.
Evaporating.

What is true is that secrets do not have to be lies.
What is true is that you have always sensed this in me. This part.
Disappearing and appearing acts with girls.

Predawn.

The blue carpet, in the former olympic ski resort gives the room
a feeling of aquarium.

In this light I am unable to rest.

You wake from an immersed castle of sleep.

We walk to a shrine whose underneath is occupied by a labyrinth.
Created by a monk centuries ago. A woman
wearing a ski jacket opens the gate.

As dawn touches the sky, we feel our way
down narrow steps. Into wooden walls
coated with layers. Residue
of tens of thousands of hands.

A continuous search for a round wheel-like lock. Beneath buildings
on earth. To find this has meant something.
A thing about heaven.

There is nothing here but blindness. A dog
shot out to drift into space. One by one the controls
shut down. How you keep talking,
your voice ordinary, winding through afternoon traffic.

Your voice ordinary as if winding through afternoon traffic.

To where the air is warm.

Reading Plato

I think about the mornings it saved me
to look at the hearts penknifed on the windows
of the bus, or at the initials scratched

into the plastic partition, in front of which
a cabbie went on about bread his father
would make, so hard you broke teeth on it,

or told one more story about the plumbing
in New Delhi buildings, villages to each floor,
his whole childhood in a building, nothing to

love but how much now he missed it, even
the noises and stinks he missed, the avenue
suddenly clear in front of us, the sky ahead

opaquely clean as a bottle's bottom, each heart
and name a kind of ditty of hopefulness
because there was one *you* or another I was

leaving or going to, so many stalls of flowers
and fruit going past, figures earnest with
destination, even the city itself a heart,

so that when sidewalks quaked from trains
underneath, it seemed something to love,
like a harbor boat's call at dawn or the face

reflected on a coffee machine's chrome side,
the pencil's curled shavings a litter
of questions on the floor, the floor's square

of afternoon light another page I couldn't know
myself by, as now, when Socrates describes
the lover's wings spreading through the soul

like flames on a horizon, it isn't so much light
I think about, but the back's skin cracking
to let each wing's nub break through,

the surprise of the first pain and the eventual
lightening, the blood on the feathers drying
as you begin to sense the use for them.

Bird Notes

i. cardinal

Though the rockabilly crest
and bandit mask
seem kinds of a kind
of avian kitsch, the deep
Benedictine red
of fall leaves and joss sticks
saturates his belly
and breast, while brown
smoke-gray threads
lightly stipple
his back, as if he too
had had to pass through
some fire, had to be saved
just to be here,
one more version of come
as you are, perched on
an owl-faced parking meter.

ii. crow

This snow is nothing.
It only simplifies what he
already knows
of branch, fence pole,
the collapsing shed
and last sore-spotted apples.
It's all the same
that the sky is ice-white
or plum-black, woodsmoke
waxing on its skin.
He has seen it all before.
He has been the one
enraged sound
on the day's unpronounced
hours, the staggering
thing someone comes to find
exterior to time.

iii. blue jay

Thought-fast, so that
what was a branch-caught
milliner's flounce
became the confectionary
opera shoe lobbed outside
to the tune of infidelity
being played inside,
the bird almost lost
into its disguise
when it rustled off
to a new branch and turned
flag for the sky,
only to turn tail again,
more hidden this time,
the shrub-snagged piece
of Persephone's dress
left to the snow and rain.

iv. hummingbird

Breaker of the sargasso
of midsummer,
beloved incidental—
a bottle-cap nest
could have contained him.
But even the dark
didn't keep his business
from continuing,
his bill's needle
singling out the lavender
while the blurred hinge
of his body and wings
steadied him.
And like the bulb
when its light goes out,
he left a blush
on the air he had occupied.

Bonnard's Garden

As in an illuminated page, whose busy edges
have taken over. As in jasmine starred
onto the vine-dense walls, stands of phlox,
and oranges, the flesh of each chilled turgid.

By herself the sleepwalking girl arranged
them: the paper airplanes now wrecked
on the vines, sodden, crumpled into blooms
which are mistaken all morning for blooms.

The paint curls out of the tubes like ointments.
In his first looking there is too much hurry.
Dandelions, irises smelling of candles.
Two clouds like legs on the bathwater sky.

Drawn out of the background green, getting
the light before everything else, the almond
tree comes forward in a white cumulus,
as though the spring had not allowed leaves.

Last night she asked what temperature arctic
water could be that beings remained in it.
Then the question brought to the blood
inside her cat, the pillow of heat on a chair.

His glimpse smudged. As in: it's about time
I made you dizzy. Here are pink grasses,
shrubs incandesced to lace, tapestry
slopes absorbing figures and birds and deer.

Nothing is lean. The lilacs have prospered
into bundles, the tulips fattened hearts.
Pelts of nasturtiums, the thicket the color of
pigeon: gray netted over the blueberry lodes.

Then the girl's scream, her finger stirring
the emerald tadpole-water, the sound
breaking into his glimpse for an instant
then subsiding to become a part of the picture.

Not the icy killing water. But the lives there,
persisting aloft. Like the wasps held in
by a shut flower at dusk, by morning released,
dusty as miners, into the restored volumes.

Occupations

Astronomer to the ten Turkish moons
counted out on your fingernails.

Surveyor to the shiny silicate scar
of the childhood cut on your brow.

Geologist to the fault-line crack
your wrist has long since healed from.

Treasurer to the coin of vaccination
darkly minted on your left arm.

Farmer to the stubbled acreage
of your chin, to the nocturnal root.

At Point Reyes

I was old. I could see this in the will
of the ocean moving in, the lavish force.

Among the seaweed were finger bones
of driftwood, some feathers, flame-blue

and teeth-white. The water was the same
as I had known it: light green within

the thinning wall of its arc, the horizon
behind it. I felt separate but unhurt,

the smallest trapeze swinging on inside
my chest. From the pieces eroded

to chalk by the sand, I had to remember
what it meant to have ruined something,

bottle after bottle cracking against rocks.
Dead things, souring in the salt air:

this was my exhaustion. The iceplants
glistened plastic pink, the poppies furled

into bullets. I started to get cold, cold
as a leaf on someone's palm. A line of

breath followed everything that I said
to myself. Somewhere in the cordgrass

I found a pair of glasses, an insect-leg
tangle of rusted wires. The sunset began

to answer the things I had my heart on:
the snowglobe city, its durable lights;

the view from a window down to wet cars,
each roof a nail painted in black polish.

American Adobo

She showed up on the doorstep of my apartment
in Albuquerque just after the blizzard of '85
in a fluffy tan fake-fur coat, an elevated

I Love Lucy hairdo, and a twelve-year-old son.
I was honored to be given the front passenger seat
of her 1976 Datsun while her son aimed

his pink plastic water pistol from the back.
Her two bedroom duplex was nestled in the foothills
of the rust-covered Sandia mountains.

The hug back at the apartment was genuine—
my older cousin, Nancy, her son, Alfonso,
named after my father. This was a chance to ignite

memories from familiar names, to recuperate
the fallen leaves of our family tree, to run
back to our childhoods, separated

by two continents and an ocean.
She said she still believes
that "the Carbós are blue-blood,

a royalty from Spain." Nobody
could take that away from her—the promise
of gold crowns, swords forged

from Toledo steel with the Carbó name
glimmering on the blade. I didn't tell her
that the only title our grandfather carried

was that of *Perito Mercantil Colegiado,* a Certified
Public Accountant. I didn't tell her that the only
time he ruled the masses was as the Vice-Mayor

of the provincial town of Nueva Caceres.
"In 1956, when I was nine,
your mother and your father came to visit

our house on Losoya Street—they came out
of a black limousine, they looked so regal,
so elegant, they brought so many gifts."

She was standing by the microwave fluffing
a pot of Uncle Ben's Minute Rice
while I reviewed her family album on the couch

which was covered with a multi-colored
Mexican blanket. I understood the story
in black and white—

her American father left them in 1954,
my aunt Nana learned to change sheets
in motels on Central Avenue and serve coffee

at diners to earn enough money
for three children. When Nana died in 1982,
Nancy was the only child to sit by her bed.

"This was my mother's special recipe
for beef and pork Adobo. She cooked it
for us on Thanksgiving and Easter Sunday."

I didn't tell Nancy that her Adobo
was too watery, that it needed more soy sauce,
that it should have had more garlic.

The Bronze Dove

1. Benigno Aquino Jr. International Airport

The adobe-brown terminal looms
like a sleeping *carabao* caked with mud—
you come up with fifty words to describe
the different shades of green you saw
rushing up from the ground,
you scratch your neck, feel the grime and sweat
from San Francisco or L.A. on your nape,
you look out your window seat
search for a plaque or a stain of blood—
this is the tarmac where he was shot.

(For a better view, go to Ayala Avenue in Makati.
In front of the Bank of the Philippine Islands
and the Insular Life Building is the statue
with the stairs and the dove on his shoulder.
While you're there, look
for the statues of Lapu Lapu and Tandang Sora
among the Ipil-ipil trees on Makati Avenue.)

You pass through a fluorescent-white curtain
of warm air as you descend
into the unloading tube—
a smile from an airline attendant,
the long walk to the Immigration booth,

Balikbayan sir? Welcome home.

a stamp for six months on your U.S. passport,
another ten dollar bill between its pages
for the Customs people up ahead,

Balikbayan? Do you have anything to declare,
pasalubong, expensive gifts
for the relatives? Thank you sir!

a porter in a red shirt takes your luggage
to the street level, asks for five dollars,
the faces of a hundred people pressed
behind a bamboo fence stare
as you board a Golden or Metro taxi cab.

You inhale the humid air, sweat is now
running down your face.

2. E. de los Santos Avenue

The Jeepnies are engorged with eight
or ten passengers, each jeepney
speeding and stopping with their fiesta
of sounds, of colors, the bodies inside
breathing carbon monoxide.

You take the overpass into Makati—
to the right is the long tan wall topped
with barbed-wire hiding the luxury homes
of Dasmarinas Village, to the left
is San Lorenzo Village where you'll find
the San Lorenzo Pre-school.
Go to the house in Zulueta Circle,
this is where the poet
of *Like The Molave* once lived.
His widow's name is Cora.

On the corner of Edsa and Buendia,
among the street vendors selling
copies of Woman's Day, Manila Bulletin,
or Marlboro and Winston cigarettes,
you might see a girl without a left arm tapping
on windows of stopped cars pointing
to her mouth, asking for money.
Every other year, before the monsoon rains,
it's the same arm that's cut off
just above the elbow, a different
young face running up to cars
in the same intersection.

3. Camp Crame and Camp Aguinaldo

You pass Camp Crame where Ninoy Aquino,
Jose Maria Sison, the poet Mila D. Aguilar,
and countless others were "detained"
under Marcos. The positive wire
attached to the penis, the negative
to the scrotum. This is also the place
where more than a million people
said "no" to the Dictator. You may still
hear stories about the tear gas,
the armored personnel vehicles,
the ordinary people who would not
move out of the way. They say
that for three days the electricity
to the whole city was turned off
but the people still fought for freedom,
sang songs to each other around bonfires,
made love by candle light.

Ang Tunay Na Lalaki Stalks the Streets of New York

looking to harvest what makes him happy.
The AA meetings have thrown
him into sacrilegious jousts with Titans

and Gorgons with glowing snake eyes
and leather pants. This is life
without the Filipino bottle,

without the star fruit boogie,
without the *bomba* films. He wears black
Dr. Martens boots because slippers

would expose his *provinciano* feet
to the snow. He wants to ride
the back of a *carabao* and bolt

up Madison Avenue screaming
like Tandang Sora or shout
hala-bira! hala-bira! hala-bira!

like his Isneg cousins in Aklan.
Ay, susmaryosep! Such bad behavior
from the "true male" of Filipino

advertising. He looks at his reflection
on a book store window, notices
that his hair has grown shoulder-length—

like Tonto in the Lone Ranger
he would watch on TV. He turns to the right,
his profile now looks like the young Bruce Lee

as Kato in the Green Hornet. Yes,
he realizes it will always be the face
of a supporting character. Rejected

from the Absolut Vodka ads, he decides
to change his name for an upcoming audition
for a Preparation H commercial—*Al Moranas,*

American but with a Filipino flare.

Ang Tunay Na Lalaki Is Baffled by Cryptic Messages

he finds on cheap match covers.

> PLEASE
> MAKE ME TASTE LIKE
> A MAN

is the first one he reads after lighting up
an American Spirit cigarette on the corner
of Broadway and Houston. The painted Statue

of Liberty on the giant DKNY ad on the side
of the building winks her big blue eye
as if she understands what those words mean,

as if she could make him taste like a man.
The street sign changes to WALK
and the natural smoke of the natural cigarette

feels good in his lungs. He thinks
of the taste of fried garlic, of anise seeds,
of rambutan fruit, of broiled tuna—

none comes close to what a man
would taste like in his mind. He reaches
underneath his shirt and sweater to scratch

his left armpit. He smells his fingers
and thinks, *this is what a Filipino man
must taste like to American women.*

To test his hypothesis, he sticks
his index finger in his mouth, pulls
it out with a slurpy sound and points upwards

as if he were testing the wind,
as if he were about to satisfy a desire,
as if he were carrying a flaming torch.

Ang Tunay Na Lalaki Visits His Favorite Painting

in the Metropolitan Museum of Art. Not
the Renoirs, the Picassos, the Van Goghs,
or the Titians—he is attracted to a watercolor

by an American, Winslow Homer's
Palm Tree, 1898. The scene is Nassau
but it could well be Cavite, Nasugbu, or Boracay

back home. The aquamarine blue
is truly tropical where one could dive in
and read the *New York Times,* watch

the lobsters and the parrot fish
look over the classifieds, or observe
a puffer fish inflate over an article

about the depletion of the rain forests.
The wind blows from right to left
in the foreground and the strips

of palm leaves agree. He can hear
the wind's missives translated
by the leaves—

barometric pressure dropping,
mostly cloudy with cumulus clouds,
something big in the air.

The red flag by the white
lighthouse in the background
blows from left to right suggesting

a circular wind. He remembers
the same conditions on Boracay island
when he looked up and saw the clear

over-heated eye of an angry typhoon.

The Sign Reads:

Unction—
        a sanctuary for the solitudes.
        Yes. I am one

too. A solitude gone
blank, the husk of my life
narrowing

into a blade. I have no
neighbors here and my neighbors
have none too.   I will pour

last night's storm
over my skin,
        catch it all

in every pore.
This rain is grief-thick.
I used to wake in my childhood home

and want my family to burn, with me
as the flame's blue dart.
They are embers now

        or could have been.
Sister pooling on the kitchen tile,
        her formless anger

forming my current burden.   Don't I lie
each time I promise
I did not leave her behind?

Swindled, I Left Everything

A town with remote reception
and hollow hills that sway like elms,
                Unction blooms one vast zero,

a mirror of my ramrod heart

lost in the collection plate's steely face.

I'm looking out a new window
only to realize it is no different: a roof's

hypotenuse, a one-armed tree, the sky

a white enormity. I hide
                only to find myself too much.

So where's
safety, where's the trail

that led me here,
that will lead me back?   *Unction* hums

parts of a song I once knew—it's
                in the wind, like a ribbon shredded loose and

feathered—I'm uncouth,
                indecipherable—*Wanting all I have lost,*

I have lost nothing.
But I have lost everything.

I imagine these words match the tune
and believe they are truth.

I Remember Her, a Bowl of Water

Here in *Unction,* thirst
is currency. I have wealth

and I have greed, my head
a pool of waves I drown in daily. I see

the walls wave too, fretting
ignorant sheets

of light. Reflection, nothing
but

a different way of looking,
I think. Or, isn't shadow

a black water, the shallow ink
we can't dive into

but want to? I remember her,
a bowl of water

I spun my loose
buttons in—a sort of

tiddlywinks—until
she spilled out and broke

the bowl. A burst
that rang like bells. Who

wiped her off the floor?
Where did she pour? Jars,

thimbles, a porcelain basin.
She ended the game. But couldn't she,

like me, have been a band
in the spectrum? A violet murmur

to my red haze? O,
she swam and she swims, treads

against currents I can't find, to the deep
where even light drowns

and water's the one uncertainty
to count on. Somewhere deeper

we will forget our faces. Sister,
here's the dress

I hand down to you—lace of algae
and brine, a sea urchin's

limy shell—hand it down
farther.

If There Is No Memory, It Did Not Happen

Mother took us
and locked us in the basement.
Sister has no memory

of this. She was, at the time,
small enough to close in a cupboard.
But the basement

was the house's dank hollow,
where the groans grew,
where we kept our yams and onions cool.

We sank into the top step
afraid to go all the way down;
there was a clucking or a whir

—*You're making it
up.*—a sound that thinned us out.
Even then I needed glasses

but would not admit it. I see the memory
in my head, only blurs. *You read
something strange in those blurs,*

*you read a story
and not the truth.* My arms slowly
disappeared so that as I grew older

I could feel nothing. *Self-pity! Whose
arms disappear? You were simply born
that way.* Mother's rages

tore off our skins. Sometimes
I was glad for myopia. How awful
we must have looked to be limbless,

skinless, and without even the vigor
to butter our toast. We ate bread dry,
like cardboard, no, we let them go

soggy in their hard heat. *There was no
toaster, no oven. Mother made wonderful
salads and after Father left, we each*

had a dozen kernels of corn at dinner.
Who looked more like Mother? A question
that gave me purpose then. I did not want

her temperament but, I think,
she had a lovely face, a wedge of moonglow
and a catalpa leaf. So I looked

carefully. I squinted because those days,
Mother was in love with our poverty
and had the celerity

of a blender. *Oh, the blurs again.* And Sister,
in adolescence, had a spinning jenny
way, a movement like grass

on a windy day. *Did you see anything?*
I saw what I saw:
Sister became watery.

What the Landscape Works For Is What I Have Left

      Is *Unction*

the cloud that covers,
                    or the cloud that passes?

A mystery, even to me.
      Am I a vapor in a vapor town

          and is Sister's memory a dew bead
forgotten on a grass blade?   White spaces, white fillers, the sky

      is the caulk that frames the cloud.   Here, with my arms,
I imitate   the birches' bleached silhouettes

      to become the thinnest grove, tracing the wind
         that dissipates,

and shapes.   I am branched
            and branchless in

this ecstasy of absence—I swallow air

until my hunger is   an insatiable question.

Then Sister was the empty bowl?
Then I was the futile drain?

I wish her on a hill   somewhere far

from the cold chambers Mother made.   A night

that rang like rage—how
do I go on?   The walls trembling or was that

a twist of light?
Mother was killing herself
or killing us.   No,

it's not that simple.
She held the blade in her small palms

not knowing how to stop the rain.   Our roof a snare drum,

it had been raining for weeks—my dreams
were of swamps and drowning,   I scorned the shower,

hid from the tub,   fearing the faucet;   that rain
should come inside.   White spaces, white fillers, the sky—

How could I stop the knocking

on the window?   Sister slept in the pantry; she believed

in cyclones. And Mother wailed with the thunder.

Really she did not know what to do
with two saucer-eyed daughters—
one licking floor dust,
the other coiled in the sheets—

so dragged us by our necks to the backyard
     and dipped us in the goldfish pond,   wailing

with the thunder.   The pond was black, the fish were gone.   I wish her

drying on the clothesline,   white as the shirts
    that fly in this wind.   Through the splash,

I could see Sister close her eyes
and swallow water, her mouth

    open as a door.   Though Mother had our hair
in fists, though I choked on rain and pond,

     a furious qualm—Sister so quiet,
   she silenced the storm.   It could be snow now

or the sky shredding a quilt.   The clouds
    are sinking down to me—could I be what holds

the mist?   Enough of this.   I avoid
    to avoid.   *Don't I?*

I *Am* in Unction *Now*

All my life   I have known
Mother stood beside a hole.

Some people carry shadows,
bad weather, but she nursed

an emptiness none of us could fill.
She liked   the pain of space

and would not let Father walk with her.
She swore she had no reflection

so our house was without
a single looking-glass. I held my hands

to my face and saw there was not much
to see anyway.   Sister cried

into her pillow
and sought a teary mirror. At night,

I said to her, we must keep   ourselves
from looking   for what isn't there. Even then,

I recognized my hypocrisy. I find everywhere
Mother's space,   the hole

deepened by regret. It is where starlings
hide their stolen eggs.   It is where

Father dropped his spectacles, took
the wrong step.   And I do not stop

to look in, to search for a dime
I have been missing twenty years.

What else have I lost? If I write a list,
I will lose the thing,   the desire

for retrieval.   So I tell myself. *Unction*
is a town of glass, not an escape.

          I am tired of the past.
I am so tired.

Origin & Ash

Powder rises
from a compact, platters full of peppermints,
        a bowl of sour pudding.
A cup of milk before me tastes of melted almonds.

It is the story of the eve of my beginning. Gifts for me:

boxes of poppies, pocket knife,
an elaborate necklace
made of ladybugs.

My skirt rushing north

There is something round and toothless
about my dolls.

They have no faith. Their mouths, young muscle
        to cut me down.
                Their pupils, miniature bruises.

I hear the cries of horses, long faces famished,

        the night the barn burned.

        God and ashes everywhere.

Burnt pennies, I loved them, I could not catch them
in their copper rolling.

My mother's cigarette burns amber in a crystal glass.
I am in bed imagining great infernos.

Ashes skimming my deep lake.

The night the animals burned,
I kissed the servant with the salty lips.

There was a spectacular explosion, a sound
that severed the nerves, I was kind
                    to that shaking. The horses,
the smell of them, like wet leaves, broken skin.

Laughing against a wall,
my hair sweeps the windowsill,

thighs show themselves.

First came my body, my statue's back, then hair electric,
          matches falling everywhere.
Tucked in my pink canopy, I am plastic,
worn cheeks grinning.

I found my little ones hiding from me,
          crying into their sleeves. They are really
from a breeze, momentary, white.

When we unburied the dolls, red ants were a fantasy
feeding on them, nest of veins, shrunken salted corpses.

There is mythology planted in my mouth which is like sin.
Keep fires inside yourself.
My mother once said, *When you were a baby,*
          I let you swim in a basin of water
until your lungs stopped. Since then, my eyes were open windows,

the year everything fell into them.

Cicadas hissing.
Ashes on my open book.

Ashes in mother's hair. Ashes on my baby brother.
The streets are arid, driven toward fire.

If I hurry, I will dance with my father before the sun sets,
my slippers clicking
on a thin layer of rain.

Invention

On an island, an open road
where an animal has been crushed
by something larger than itself.

It is mangled by four o'clock light, soul
sour-sweet, intestines flattened and raked
by the sun, eyes still watchful, savage.

This landscape of Taiwan looks like a body
black and blue. On its coastline mussels have cracked
their faces on rocks, clouds are collapsing

onto tiny houses. And just now a monsoon has begun.
It reminds me of a story my father told me:
He once made the earth not in seven days

but in one. His steely joints wielded lava and water
and mercy in great ionic perfection.
He began the world, hammering the length

of trees, trees like a war of families,
trees which fumbled for grand gesture.
The world began in an explosion of fever and rain.

He said, Tina, your body came out floating.
I was born in the middle of monsoon season,
palm trees tearing the tin roofs.

Now as I wander to the center of the island
no one will speak to me. My dialect left somewhere
in his pocket, in a nursery book,

a language of childsplay. Everything unfurls
in pictures: soil is washed from the soles of feet, a woman
runs toward her weeping son, chicken bones float

in a pot full of dirty water.
I return to the animal on the road.
When I stoop to look at it

it smells of trash, rotting vegetation,
the pitiful tongue. Its claws are curled tight
to its heart; eyes open eyes open.

When the world began
in the small factory of my father's imagination
he never spoke of this gnarled concoction

of bone and blood that is nothing like wonder
but just the opposite, something
simply ravaged. He too would die soon after

the making of the world. I would go on
waking, sexing, mimicking enemies.
I would go on coaxed by gravity and hard science.

Fish Story

It is the hour of news. The television cracks
its voice over the radiator and the blue carpet. Always
that same cooked silver of you, oil spilling
from the mouth, ginger and scallions burning

through the scales. My father thinks you are delicate
as he steals the eggs from the purse
of your belly, white interior exposed and steaming.
I think of you breathing before the slipping out.

You once slept on a bed of light and cracked shells.
Jellyfish swelled around your eyes. Your body weaved
through coral. Cold blood stained the air when you were caught,
the snails and the clouds erasing. Netting grasped

the whole of you, the back bending so completely,
it could snap as water escaped your yellow heart.
Rubber tires and shrimp, green glass and mollusks
were caged with you. I know how painful it can all be:

The blade and the quick gutting,
the aroma of yourself frying in a smoky haze,
your body covered with radishes and leafy greens.
This activity of eating brains is real.

The knowledge of abalone, barracuda, the stingray
can be transferred by licking the flowers
from inside the skull of a fish. The bowl of the sea
and all its blue water, amphibians, salty mammals

can be absorbed in one swallow. And so my father does this
with hope. As his sight diminishes he pushes
out your eyes with his thumb,
you see the dry, contained world in this white

room before he sucks you down. This is the last
of the swimming, the final melting of fin and gills,
life broken down by the sallow tongue and feverish saliva,
the salt and sauce defeating you.

Versions

It is the middle of January
in the year I am trying to remember.
I'm in a small red jacket with
mittens clipped to the sleeves.
The mittens are attachment
which means the father never left.
My stained lips breathe a white haze.

Now my brother is laughing,
but maybe he is screaming
and I must reach him through
the snow. In another version,
he is sitting beneath a willow tree,
holding his wounded leg and there
is no one to help him. The wind chills
the interior of my lungs
as I watch him, broken.

My mother is inside believing
in safety as she puts bones into broth.
She has all the makings of a mother
but in another version she throws
everything into the refrigerator
and forgets. The tiny hearts of
strawberries go frosted with rot.

I am fatherless which means
the father is in another room,
hiding where no one else but myself
can see. This game of hide and seek
when I am a girl is dangerous. Danger
forms my own weightlessness, forgetfulness.
The fact that I've studied the weather
tells me the snow never stops. The snow
that never stops means a story with no end,
meaning a character with absolute grief.

Curriculum

1: Prowess

Walk into a room a high priestess.
Inherit fortune through the mouth.
Feel God's hand reaching down
to place a gift on your tongue
like a fresh coin. Swallow.
This is how you take it: bread, light,
a vantage point in the heart.

2: Stamina

Keep going when lungs are shriveled,
two bags of bad air. The professor sleeps
in a suit, makes ready with a suitcase
by the door and a wife
at his elbow. Wake up early,
wake up dying.

3: Render

A young girl brushes her hair
till she aches. Her father stole a chicken from a neighbor.
As punishment the town priest takes
the daughter as his slave. Every night he pushes
the curtains back, crawls on top of her
small body. He forgives and is forgiven.

4: Contempt

The heart is something daily slain.
The man is happy who goes off
to war, kills fields full of children,
becomes a hero. He returns, axing
the thin white flowers of his walls.
Then offers himself to his family,
quietly, an earful of bullets.

5: Change.

I was once a gnat, then a gardener,
then a fallen saint. Each time I am new again,
failing by flying, then
by drowning. The nuns waft by
in their habits whispering of the criminal
who got it real good. My skin is molting,
an inky blue. When I shed, I come out clean.

Journal of the Diabetic Father

I.

I'm a stack of newspapers.
A kettle. A plate left out to dry.
Scanning the classifieds,

I lose myself in the alphabet.
Falling asleep between the letters,
black print stains my eyes.

II.

My mother wears paper roses in her wig.
Winter, in the kitchen, mice eat their way
through air to reach a nest of bananas.

There is nothing to do but let them go.
She tells me to talk to no one.
I talk to no one. Once I reach the roof

I read a Cantonese mystery.
The children below run,
breaking the windows with sticks.

III.

They call my father King of Burned Pots
as he stands before columns of dishes
in the back of the restaurant,

his arms immersed in brown water,
pork grease and mussel shells.
Hidden behind a veil of white steam

he is washing, always washing.
And I imagine the width
his tired shoulders.

IV.

I'm under the sink fixing a leak.
Tap water slides across my wrist:
chicken fat, hair, water.

The wrench falls out of my grasp.
The disease has taken me
not by the throat but the hands.

V.

Could there be anything better
than transforming myself
into a boat or a komodo dragon,

forgetting my sickness
and gorging on a bowl of ice cream
and the hundred cashews I adore?

The room smells of alcohol, Tiger Balm,
dried rags. I am sick, sick in the knees.
A cup of rice and a prune for breakfast.

Unemployment has me cooking
the broad beans, overwatering
the rhododendrons, flapping

my slippers on the basement steps.
Lord, no one is listening to me.
The grocer changes beef prices daily.

VI.

My sons are tapping on my door in a dream.
All of them wait for me in a plush corridor.
My wife dresses me in fine trousers.

I'm laughing in front of a long table
of turkey and apples. When I wake,
the house is vacant.

VII.

The sugar is taking effect.
It is burning me up, raising my ashes
to the god I wish I could be.

All over my body
an atlas of wounds, my mouth
a street corner, a reservoir.

Manong Jose, While Cleaning His Last Window before Coffee, Sees Fidelito and Is Pleased Though Wary

They've come off the plane like so many spent and dirty rags I've used on airport windows, split, threadbare and dim. But it's good to see folks from the old country. She with her three hand-carry bags, probably all she owns. He with the look of a bruised warrior, or a man unsure of his footstep after being set adrift too long. Then there's the boy.

That kid there is a rough one. He looks beautiful and misunderstood like martyrs. All aura and golden, though pierced with the spit of the faithless. Yes, he's a rough one who carries himself with too much purpose for a child his age. I feel the pull of the moon in him. It's in the way he wears his hair, the cowlick up, forever ascending . . .

When Fidelito Is the New Boy at School

He is a frequent eclipse . . . a shadow on fire. The light breaks over the schoolyard and a hallucination of evenly cropped trees in stride moves the glass. As the dusk forms of spruce pass his face, he disappears.

He keeps his mouth shut and his palms open despite the steady drum of spit-wads, kid-song, and the long clock's nervous face. Bells refuse to breathe. And the wide hours wait for doors to open.

Fidelito gazes outside. There are other milder distractions: some of the children eat their shirts and some burst into rain. A road burns into a corner. In the power lines above the playground, a grackle's steel eye murders the earth. And the sky, now perfect for flight, is open like the older mouth of our moon.

Grounding

At noon the cloud-plume's whorled face divides the sky, weather
unstable for flight. So Fidelito, sullen and gray, fills a stiff chair by the
window and sulks like a salty rag. Swimming, water streaks the glass . . .

Fidelito, looking out angrily, admires stars. They can't resist drawing
their wings back inside the storm's mouth. He wonders—what now that
winds pull the hair of trees? Then the rain. Its hollow fingers strum
against the roof.

Poor Fidelito. How children drown in the language of thundershowers.
Now, he thinks, mockery is being made of him, grounded. The rain
gutters pool long necklaces of sound, making asphalt gleam.
Somewhere, Fidelito thinks, the stars and their shrouded eyes peer into
his dry house.

Carpenter Ants

Maria Elena thought she had left her troubles with the armored ones in
another country. But they are here, crouched between boards of the side
porch among viny undergrowth. Whole legions of them. So Maria Elena
guards the door, various cracks in the house, drafty windows.

The world is no longer her own. A sudden ring of the phone goes
unanswered for fear of invasion. Poisons sprinkled around the house
curl about the rooms like an embarrassed nude. But they don't work.
So, prompted by memory, Maria Elena opens every door. She prays the
old prayers and watches them drift with the fumes about the house. The
television fills the air with rain.

The ants are prepared. Underneath, where the boards touch ground,
they churn up earth. They sing songs for wood. They lay blueprints
before their armies. They celebrate blight and dying, wedged into the
grains of two-by-fours like a blood clot, like a clump in the brain.

Nine Secrets the Recto Family Can't Tell the Boy

The Mole of Maria Elena's Armpit

Roughly the size of a quarter. Her husband calls it her beautiful armpit. Once with Domingo, she wore a sleeveless shirt to the grocery store— just once. Before patrons could stare at her as she reached for a can of peas, he slid a hand under her arm. Now she has two wardrobes: "Public" and "Private."

Love Postcards

There are three of them. When Domingo is away he's not one for words. On the back of a portrait of the Columbia River, it reads, 'Gone Fishing.' The self-critical one from Seattle reads, 'I've just realized how much I hate the weather here and it saddens me.' The insightful third: a buxom blonde sends greetings from Venice Beach with Domingo's note, 'You can't live here without wheels.'

Overheard Long-Distance Phone Conversation

'You mean you can't distinguish between a lychee and a longan?' Cost: six-dollars.

The Boy's Ears

They think Fidelito gets them from great grandfather Carlos on Maria Elena's side, the way they stick out like an awning. He was the talk of the barrio then. On hot days, people paid him to turn circles and circulate the air. Saturday nights, the people would say, 'Meet you under Carlos,' and huddle under his earlobe. Often, they used him to eavesdrop on conversations. At one point, he was the most hated man in Luzon.

The Pearls

They're glass, of course. Domingo was poor. Maria Elena with a pencil, sometimes runs the eraser-end along the grooves while her husband sits in front of the television. It distracts him. He thinks she's unzipping the back of her dress and chopping onions in the nude.

The Inherited Autographed Photo

It's of Sophia Loren in her younger days, playing her role as Dulcinea. Domingo keeps it locked away in a safety deposit box at the bank. Her hair, tied back, wants to roam. The red dress she clutches twirls into the script of her 'Sophia.' When he thinks of her, Domingo hums in adagio.

The Bag of Soil

It was from under the house where Maria Elena was born. She and her husband also lived thereuntil the boy was born. She keeps it in her stocking and underwear drawer. The corpses of three ants float in and out when she shakes the bag. She thinks, when she dies, this shall be the first earth thrown on her casket.

The Matchbook

A reminder that Domingo quit smoking when Fidelito was born. Now, in every restaurant or hotel, he seeks them. One matchbook has a picture of Aurora Diamond on the inside flap, a one-time headliner for the Topless Girls of Glitter Gulch. He keeps it apart from the others. On the cover a blue boot moves when tilted, and the small print says 'Keep your spurs on, cowboy.'

A Night on the Town

Some Saturday evenings, they leave Fidelito at home with the baby-sitter. He does not hear where his parents are going, despite the largeness of his ears. Domingo makes reservations for dinner with Maria Elena at a seafood restaurant along the wharf. She wears her white 'Private' labeled spaghetti strapped dress, and faux-pearls. Her hair tightly braided in a long black rope drapes over her shoulder, covering her armpit. Domingo drives with the window rolled down and puffs away at a Cremosa lit by Aurora Diamond. They descend on the Embarcadero to soft operetta. And in the moonlight, the smell of the ocean and stars.

Marisa de los Santos

Rite of Passage

Wrong, the belief we'd called you into the world.
You broke like a seal, almond-eyed and slick,
from a body as anonymous as ocean.

In the months preceding, we'd countered mystery's
presence with invention. Your father conjured
a cartwheeling star, laughing infant tipping

toward us, end over end through space. Baffled
into reverence, I pictured you wise, a tiny monk
wrapped in quiet and saffron and red. We joked,

but believed we'd caught the spirit of you.
Not joyous or peaceful, fierce creature,
seconds old, you lay on my chest and howled,

spreading and fisting raised hands against
the new light, beating it back, tugging it in.
I saw to what end I'd labored: not delivery,

but deliverance, yours. *In labor* they say; *in*,
as though pain were a room or water or fog.
In deep, I named it *a wilderness of pain.*

Thin, unspectacular metaphor, but I said it
over and over, shot it up like a flare I used
to locate myself, black-haired woman on the bed.

Now, weeks later, time snags nightly on the nail
of your hard crying. I never imagined such nights
—arid, comfortless—your cries resembling only

what they are, angry animal shouts, sound
so absolute it cancels out thought and words
like *mother*. Holding you, I feel myself erased.

(To think *erased* is failure, to write it, betrayal.
But do I love you? While you sleep, I measure
an hour by your quick breaths, another

by your thin scalp's pulse. What word is there
for this? In your absence, my arm bones grieve,
my breasts weep milk. What counts as love?)

I should have seen my disappearance coming.
The story of your birth didn't end with birth
as I'd expected: weary but blissful mother;

swabbed baby sleeping in a white gown,
a pretty couplet to snap the sonnet shut.
Instead, after a brief reprieve, the jagged dance

began again, proof of relativity: time expanding
each time I contracted to a hot, red point.
I bled too much, nothing pretty about that.

Hemorrhage. The word itself is ugly, thick,
messy with its silent second *h,* containing rage.
My blood pressure dropped rapidly toward

no soft landing. As your father waited with you
in the nursery, they wheeled me toward surgery.
Voices coaxed, "Keep talking. Tell us your name,"

and reluctantly I gave it to them, the syllables
smooth and solid as a fistful of pearls. Round
lights burned like moons and then went out.

I awoke to you in your father's arms, hungry,
drinking from a dropper. Marked by blood
and fear, this turned out to be a just initiation.

Those hours spoke the harsh and blessed truth,
saying to me, "Let there be no confusion.
Of the two, yours is the expendable life."

October: One Year Later

He takes the long way through her
state, keeps to the valley's farm roads
and empty two-laners. Silos dazzle
in afternoon light. He's missed this:

rickrack fences weathered to pewter
and bone, wide, pillared porches, churches
and battlefields with their plaques,
their solitary stone soldiers.

People here take such pains to keep
the past intact. He thinks of yearly
mendings, fresh paint, the patching
of plaster and brickwork, all the patient

labor of hands. And he has to get back
to the highway where he won't see
how the mountains are bluing
like bruises, how she was that single

red tree—a plume of sparks
among the green—how this landscape's
beauty can sting like the burst
from an orange at the first dig
of fingernails, the first pulling back.

First Light

I shake the night rains loose from sapling oaks
to catch the water on my face. The smooth
trunks cool my palms. Beneath the morning's

clear, amazing corals, magnolia
blossoms do their slow unscrolling. Touch,
however light, would scar, and so I keep

myself from handling petals I know would
feel something like my lover's skin:
his inner wrists, the hollow of his throat.

The woman—thin, dark-haired—who loved him last
spring called at 2 A.M., her time. A whole
year gone and she's not finished wanting him

to suffer. When he spoke to her, his voice
was not his voice, was pavement cracking in
unseasonable cold, so I got dressed

and walked outside. It's good to be this way,
alone and thinking, "Vivid, vivid!" I
would use my hands to gather up and knot

the corners of this morning. The screen door
creaks. He says my name three times, the third
time softly, so I turn and walk inside.

When we're in bed the sun, now up, is white,
the floor, the walls, our bodies bleaching, as
my careful movements rip his breath to rags.

Because I Love You,

I cannot tell you that last night in the exhaust-
fume impatience of nearly-stopped traffic
through which cars crept, linked
with short chains of light,
the driver at my front failed for whole minutes
to follow closely the blue Buick in front of him,
stopped, in fact, entirely, while a thousand
engines idled in molasses-sticky Virginia heat.

I caught the fine, still cut-out of his face
as he leaned a little out the window, looking,
so I turned, too, and saw what I had missed in long
minutes of waiting: a bank of cloud like descending
birds, a great, bright raspberry moon,
and I was surprised into loving this man as I
have loved others—ancient-eyed boys reading on benches,
crossing guards in white gloves,
businessmen sleeping on trains—easily,
as I have never loved you.

Woman Reading

> after a Japanese wood cut
> of the early 19th century

A flow of water, a flowering tree,
unbroken eggwhite light. There's something here

I want and think I've lost. It's not the spot
itself although it's one I might have chosen.

I like lake winds and morning reading, how
new blossoms seem to burn a thin black branch:

redbud, dogwood, ornamental cherry.
I've seen such spots before. I've even seen

such light, though rarely. What illumination
I have known has been mostly shaded

bulbs, porch lamps, the sputter of fireflies low
above cut lawns. Still, that strange light is not

the thing I miss. What's left to look at is
the woman reading, wrapped in silk, alone.

And there it is. Not the woman really.
With her tiny birdwing hands and face

as blank as linen, she is nobody
I know. It's got to do with how alone

she looks, alone as I've forgotten how
to be. I've found a man I'm sure I'm glad

I love, and now when anybody speaks,
I hear the way the voice is unlike his.

I watch my own hand turn a page and see
my fingers fanned across his chest. I met
him in September. In two days, it will be June.

Brian Komei Dempster

Measure

Uncle, did I come to see you as only half a man
with your shaved head and lead blanket,
half the weight, half the breath, half the smile,
only half of you looking at the doctor
who loaded up the transparency, used a ruler
to show the tumor, its increments,
this angle, 70%, that angle 50%, back at half
again, in this case, your chance of living.
1 set of x-rays needed, a 2nd opinion, a 3rd, each
arbitrary as the 4 vertebrae swarmed
by the 4,123 diseased cells, the 7,000
blood count, 5,126 swollen lymphs,
and the fact that there were 3 doctors,
6 orderlies, 9 interns only made calculations
trickier. 2 options: 48 weeks of radiation
or 12 hours under the knife. 3 pills a day
after either treatment. Within 1 year
a 50% chance to live. A 250,000
deductible to cover cost after the 8th week.
1 oxygen tank and cane for full recovery.
The 1 opaque streak vanishing from
the transparency. The 2 cigars we smoked
to celebrate. Our 1 hour tennis match,
the score 6–3 because you didn't want
any measure of pity, my 5 aces, your 4 double
faults, no strategy against the 3 opaque streaks
growing back into the transparency. The 29 steps
to your room where I tied the white laces
of your gown. The 1 tuna fish sandwich

I brought you Sunday, the 7th, at 8 P.M.,
2 bites while you looked out the window
at 2 sparrows darting back and forth, warbling
atop 1 branch, a single pine cone falling.

Exposure

In the movie, a woman sits in front of a mirror,
watching her hair fall out.

My hand searches the bag between Amber's legs.

My fingertips are butter and salt when I lick them,
and when the camera pans to the right side of the woman's head,

I cringe at the single bald spot.

Is exposed flesh the reason she fiddles
with the lock of the varnished box?

The booth projects the beam

of my father's flashlight, leading us beneath
the porch, down a ladder, through a maze of pipes,

to an entrance where he clears away cobwebs.

And this woman is my mother in photos
after the war, dressed in a kimono,

u-shaped pins propping her hair, her face powdered with talc.

Where is the key to unlock this box?
A bomb shelter my father calls it. Night after night

I climb under the covers while he descends

beneath the house, the tip of his shovel ticking
against the earth like a metronome.

And during the drills, when I crawl under my desk,

I turn to him, down on his hands and knees
as he tape measures length and depth, arranges

the brick into rows to trowel with mortar.

Our secret place he calls it. Amber and I
are hidden away like his jugs of water and boxes

of powdered eggs, the air black as her mother's frock.

Perhaps the cross beneath Amber's sweater
is why I harden alone inside my jeans, why I want

to unknot the sash of the woman on screen, to explore

each scar she soothes with aloe,
each blemish of my father who shucks off

his plaid shirt and boots while I peek through a crack in the door.

And the woman lifts the veil of hair, exposing
another bald spot; is she why I leave the theater,

turn away from Amber in some abandoned lot?

I've forgotten if the woman finds the clip
or if the box remains locked,

and whether this was my mother who used to sit

this same way, combing out knots
with her pearl-handled brush.

The hairpin she picks up has a butterfly,

carved into silver, veined with chartreuse
and magenta. Now the naked patch

is the blank screen, and I think it's my father

who finds the right one,
to pin back her hair like a curtain.

The Pink House in Four Variations

The Babysitter Mother:

My son's hands prick like scaled fish, his bedroom door
latched. His hush to the boys, his tongue sharp on the girls
who reel like pinballs inside machines. In my hands
I thread their silence, my needle sealing the holes.

Her Son:

The children's pinned wrists, shaping them into a cross.
A bed dressed in tattered sheets, my voice of wine,
the finger I raise to my lips. Their raven prayers,
my stubble blossoming over them like thorns.

His Sister:

I am leaking inside a tub, my mother sews
a quilt of tomatoes. In the next room
I hear the children counting songbirds
my brother strangles in their throats.

Us, the Children:

We are steaks on a board, freezing the son's blade.
Our mouths his well filling with dirt and piss. Grass,
bugs fucking upside down. Between our teeth, his cock
riveting. The throat shreds the heart into songbirds.

The Burning

I.

Our babysitter bathes our tongues
in Tabasco, five spoonfuls
when we break a dish,

ten when we scream
above the TV. The burning tells us
don't ask why

each time her son leads us
down the stairs.
His hands sit us side by side.

My lids slit open
to his glass tank of orange scales,
the weight

of turquoise water.
Zipper seams click.
No, links of the garage door

opening. A voice skids
into his palm. No, a tricycle
squealing. It may be

Salsa Brava, Picante.
Maybe she feeds us drops,
not spoonfuls.

II.

The walls fuzz
with whiskey shots,
chips are dipped

into something hot.
Salsa, definitely not Tabasco.
Through mouthfuls of ice

the burn brings back our story.
Don't say anything you say to me.
I kiss you. No, you kiss

me. Jeans drop
to the floor, then your skirt.
Come closer his voice

echoes, you move me
Closer you breathe in
as I enter the form

of you . . . *come* away
from your palms pressing
against his cage of muscle . . .

here where my hands guide
your lips, I bring you *closer*
to say my name.

III.
I idle at the pink house
with peeling white trim,
the babysitter long gone.

Behind the chainlink tangled
with helixes of ivy,
a radiator lays on its side,

leaking rust into the yard.
As I turn the corner,
the rearview mirror catches

the son's window, a sheet
drawn taut over the pane.
In the heat we grow still.

The chain of his door
locks us into place,
our bodies dissolving

inside the black room.
Don't tell anyone. A goldfish
gurgles, trapped in the light.

The son unzips,
he burns through us
until all warmth is gone.

The Fox Hole

"Oh great," she yells, "a fox hole!" and jumps right in. And just in time, too, because a shell immediately explodes a few feet away, throwing a clump of dirt on her head. She is bunched up like a mummy, but not too uncomfortable, a woman in the flush of youth squatting in a ready-made fox hole. Another shell explodes, this time even closer, and throws more dirt on her head. She is almost completely buried. There's dirt in her nose, in her eyes, in her mouth. A soldier could walk right over her and not notice that here, just beneath his feet, is a pretty woman squatting in a fox hole. But then she realized that she had been sitting on something. Something sinewy, bunched up. Was it a root? A hand? A hand grenade?

The Most Beautiful Word

I think "vesicle" is the most beautiful word in the English language. He was lying face down, his shirt burnt off, back steaming. I myself was bleeding. There was a harvest of vesicles on his back. His body wept. "Yaw" may be the ugliest. Don't say, "The bullet yawed inside the body." Say, "The bullet danced inside the body." Say, "The bullet tumbled forward and upward." Light slanted down. All the lesser muscles in my face twitched. I flipped my man over gently, like an impatient lover, careful not to fracture his C-spine. Dominoes clanked under crusty skin: Clack! Clack! A collapsed face stared up. There was a pink spray in the air, then a brief rainbow. The mandible was stitched with blue threads to the soul. I extracted a tooth from the tongue. He had swallowed the rest.

Earth Cafeteria

Mudman in earth cafeteria,
I eat aardwolf. I eat ant bear.
I eat mimosa, platypus, ermine.

"White meat is tasteless, dark meat stinks."
(The other white meat is pork, triple X.)

Rice people vs. bread people.
White bread vs. wheat bread.
White rice vs. brown rice.
Manhattan vs. New England.
Kosher sub-gum vs. knuckle kabob.

"What is patriotism but love of the foods one had as a child?"*

To eat stinky food
is a sign of savagery, humility,
identification with the earth.

"It was believed that after cleaning, tripe still contained ten percent
        excrement which was
therefore eaten with the rest of the meal."**

Today I'll eat Colby cheese.
Tomorrow I'll eat sparrows.
Chew bones, suck fat,
bite heads off, gnaw on a broken wing.

Anise-flavored beef soup smells like sweat.
A large sweaty head bent over
a large bowl of sweat soup.

---

 * Lin Yutang
** Mikhail Bakhtin

A Pekinese is ideal, will feed six,
but an unscrupulous butcher
will fudge a German shepherd,
chopping it up to look like a Pekinese.

Toothless man sucking
a pureed porterhouse steak
with straw.

Parboiled placenta.

To skewer and burn meat is barbaric.
To boil, requiring a vessel, is a step up.

To microwave.

People who eat phalli, hot dogs, kielbasas
vs. people who eat balls.

To eat with a three-pronged spear and a knife.
To eat with two wooden sticks.
To eat with the hands.

Boiling vs. broiling.

To snack on a tub of roasted grasshoppers at the movies.

Longitudes

Walking for several lifetimes, we finally reached that country.
A city at the end of a 24 hour bus ride.
A walk across the street.
Oakland by the Seine.
The Trenton of the East.
The skyscrapers resembled adobe huts from afar,
And a well-paved road appeared as a river.
I ordered food by gesturing,
And asked for directions by gesturing,
And watched TV inside a well-lit coffin.
The earth is our stewardship, the dung beetle declared.
This far below the mirror's surface,
Only cowards can survive.
I've lived my whole life by this speed bump, Sir,
And know every nook of this stinking alley.
A provincial often thinks himself superior to a cosmopolitan
Because he knows every nook of a stinking alley.
And I've been married for a century to this fire hydrant.
My dream is to travel to the dim continent,
If only for an afternoon.
Someday soon I hope to return
To the hamlet of the dozing fathers,
Where porch swings provide easy refuge
From the cares of the day,
And the movie house shows cartoons on Saturday.

Persephone

1.

Mother, I love you. But with the dead
we drink differently, holding the cup
in the left hand, pouring the wine *this* way
into our mouths. Please understand.
What we do not say, I still mean;
the sound of purple drowns those other words out.

2.

Oh, Mother, there is so much time, you
can't imagine it: sand slipping through
a needle's eye. Dead seconds fall and
fall through earth like single leaves.
Do you want to know about the lost?
Plum-colored petals floating on the deep.

3.

Yes, I ate them. I don't remember
how they tasted, only the moment
before: those six seeds held out to me
pearly, translucent, almost *singing*.
All I need to do is close my eyes
to feel the world streaming under my feet.

4.

Pull down your arrow from the bow: you see
I have grown used to that other sun.
Here even your sweetest fruit shrivels,
half of every flower is shadow.
All your other children die: but I
am the stillness in a frozen star.

5.

He calls me his obsidian angel;
I am an adamantine queen
on a throne of silver. Now do you see?
What kind of girl would wear an iron crown?
I believe it was always there
in my nature; perhaps you were afraid to speak.

6.

I hear him ringing my hour. Someday
I will tell you about falling, and what
rises out. Don't always wish for *otherwise:*
I have had enough of always, for now.

Once I was too glad:
this world does not permit such things.

In the Grips of a Sickness Transmitted by Wolves

Sorrento, at night the long fingers of your orange lights
Prick me in the sizzling streets, where the pinnacles
Of other people ring tinny and papier-mâché. Is this the way
Up to the murderous cliff? It's most important that I get there
And leave no witness. Ah, is this the majolica medallion
Which marks the grave of girl abducted by a stallion
Whom she gave a lump of maple sugar?

For that was in an autumn,
The time of year when young girls get hopeless and feel like
Giving it all away, the way a matronly merchant
Might brush off her lap, at the iron end of the market day:
It's over, it's worthless, without deserving and without
Purpose have I nourished this hope in my small patch of earth,
A sickly weed whose nodding sun's gone nova.

In the Binary Alleys of the Lion's Virus

Sorrento, your sun is light yellow lemonskin, your sky
Purling out like a farther surf on which I ride away
From that secret in a German town. I left behind
A dragon of enigma to fester there without me, I left
A small god ticking like a time bomb: a tiny jade statue suspended
By magnets in the vulva of a prehistoric temple. Here
In the oyster of your mornings I wake as lead.

Once I was a knight
Who rode out in search of grail, now I am just a husk
Of armor with the grey squid of memory inside—I have forgotten
Land and tongue, I have forgotten everyone. Only I see
An emblem, some kind of lion arrant on ash-argent ground
A creature I greeted once in a dream: yes, at the crossroads of the
hallowed grove
He kissed me—and must have slipped this curse between my lips.

Despair: The Fire of Despair

To flux the snakebite I swallowed the whole
Vial of venom. Presently, vapored and fevered, I
Became the queen who lies on her lion-footed couch
Sweating into the light white sheet of day.

—Everyone is whispering behind a think screen:
They speak of her *pulse,* her *signs of vitality,* her *blood
Pressure,* the awful bolus of its squeezing
Far too much red stuff into far too small a pump.

Now the fires are all gone out. For three days I have been ash:
On the fourth the slightest wind can blow me to pieces:
A scrap of a smile, shred of the has-been-girl clinging
Like remnants of a sail scattered on the blank sea.

Cathy Park Hong

All the Aphrodisiacs

blowfish arranged on a saucer. Russian roulette. angelic slivers.

ginseng. cut antlers allotted in bags. dogs on a spit, a Dutch girl

winking holding a bowl of shellfish.

white cloth, drunkenness. a different language leaks out—
the idea of throat, an orifice, a cord—

you say it turns you on when I speak Korean.

The gold paste of afterbirth, no red—

Household phrases　　　　　—*pae-go-p'a*　(*I am hungry*)
　　　　　　　　　　　　　—*ch'i-wa*　　(*Clean up*)
　　　　　　　　　　—*kae sekki*　(*Son of a dog*)

I breathe those words in your ear which make you climax,
afterwards you ask me for their translations. I tell you it's a secret.

gijek niin tigit rril—the recitation of the alphabet; gutteral dipthong,
　　gorgeous.

What are the objects that turn me on: words—

han-gul: the language first used by female entertainers, poets,
　　prostitutes.

The sight of shoes around telephone wires, pulleyed by their laces, the
    blunt word cock.

little pink tutus in FAO Schwarz,
they used to dress me as a boy when I was four.

white noise, white washed. the whir of ventilation in the library.

even quarantined amongst books, I tried to kiss you once. Tried to
    touch your cock.

Strips of white cotton, the color of the commoner, the color of virtue,
the color that can be sullied—

my hand pressed against your diaphragm, coralling your pitch,

a pinch of rain caught between mouths,

analgesic, tea. poachers drawing blood—

strips of white cotton I use to bind your wrist to post, tight
enough to drawl vein, allow sweat—

sweat to sully the white of your sibilant body,

the shrug of my tongue, the shrug of command, *ssshhht.*

Assiduous Rant

Here is a morning when English
is gibberish so *blue* is *blur* or *bliss;*

Mother assembles dolls in the assembly line,
works at a shoe store, then she stops working;

Flowers belie a smooth mitosis in green houses,
the sun is a constant x in the equation of silence;

I draw lopsided gowns and cheer for the giant's death.

When I finally understand English, a classmate cups
her hands around my ear. I am eager for the tender

secret and she screams gibberish in my ear.

'What is this, a Korean parade?' the obese pale man
cries to the rag tag circle of skinned kneed kids.

I save my words for a cold, indecipherable day.
Think of acidic quips years after the attack.

The source is the gorging mouth, the tale
half-told: the giant was Indian,

The king kidnapped him and had him
macerated for his whale-like bones.

guernica was an overheard cry,

Now there is uncertainty, a feast of all mouths.
A need to get heard,

my throat burns from lucidity, bellowing "3
ellipses not 4, N dash not M!"

The giant was Indian. The king kidnapped him
and burned him for his exaggerated bones.

Gibralter was a homeless black man with a sock
full of pennies, terrorizing a subway full of passengers until
a Puerto Rican woman calmly sat down. He called her
a whore and she calmly said, "yo breath stinks. You needs
a tic tac." And he calmed down.

During Bath

I am an old man in my fantasies, a darting pupil, a curious ghost.

Two catacombic bodies: legs, arms, salamander
tongues, their skin is fair.

Sometimes they are in a field colored by autumn,
a garden knitted by cabbage, stakes of fat tomatoes.

Sun that marks their leonine shapes—
the scent of pink cunt and lemon verbena.

Now it is just me in a large room with all the dolls
I used to own, stacked like bags of flour.

Or I am in the bath, taking the shape of Marat.
My arm slung over the ledge like iced fish,

water that is less warm, a sideshow shadow,
my own darker skin.

The tongue to mid palate. Coiled to the back of your teeth,
tighten your throat muscle. Utter a low pitch, exhale.

There is no room to exhale.

My parents did not dare moan, not even breathe for fear
of waking their children.

Palpitation, cyst, polyp: the parts of skin that are not
discussed; much more accepted is skin as cartography.

Why is it only words that I think of?
It is not my hand that touches his face, but a hand,

the mark on his face that does not last a second
though I want it to singe.

To first write the words:
undressed, blueprint, revolver.

Return to the bath: the loaves of my breasts, navel,
blood rush. I am not anemic. Repeat

rose, paen, fuck: to first write the words.

Not Henry Miller but Mother

Passion is the letter "p." A jeweled pear, another guernica shattering our souls, a giant liced with lilliputians. Passion fell flat on its face when a date used too much tongue. Passion ran, shotput into the air past the scoreboard, past the empty lots where children brawled silently, past the manicured lawns of Silicon Valley's royalty and past my sweaty, consumptive grasp. Following the flock, I traveled to Europe and scaled the Catalan steps to view a landscape of stone. It was cold, I left early. Later in Paris, I searched for passion in the vessel of a French man and only found a janitor who cleaned the toilets of Notre Dame and whispered "I have many, *many* faults."

She was the one who hoarded passion. Mother, who shaved my head when I was three, who dieted on tears and Maalox, who shouted in hyena rage and one minute later, cradled my face and whispered a song in my ear, while I watched the clock ahead of me, ticking.

Antonio Jocson

Lot's Wife

Look—can you blame her?
Up ahead expanses of uncertainty, scorpion
darting in the rock piles, rock shade, no place
for her head. Sweetheart, she might say
to the haunches caked with dust,
trembling so that a soul might live.
Sweetheart—her syntax, syllables fall among
roadside rubble, no one to turn to, not an angel
in the pure world, grass under her feet
as she hurries away from the airborne
noise of attack in the poisoned distance.

The seconds propagate in her mind:
first into lichen, then weed, then leaf, then shade
at the foot of her dwelling, husband at her bed,
her daughters—Each second scorches her,
breaks into color, she need not even shut her eyes
to command the endless reminiscence shining
like firework, beckoning, wind over golden meadow.
Her feet stumble on infested rocks, her voice
over the heat-bitten green of the lord, each wick
of grass consumed with obedience as her steps
crush them. Sweetheart—he will not look at her.

At the gates now of the little place, ants
setting fire to a stony carcass; the sun,
furious over the land, overthrows the ground
with shadows, strangers at the battlements
and wells—Her husband's feet are dusty,
he has spoken with the lord, working that
which is unseemly. He has long decided,
forgetting the natural use of the woman
who calls on after him as he burns in his lust
toward something else. What good
is the future if the lord follows us into it?

What did she want to last, and not be erased
so swiftly, irrevocably? Now nothing to return to,
all the lust burning in evidence, recompense
for error. What is error? Mere disobedience?
On her husband's shirtback there must have been
an iridescence persuading her, ghost in the soaked
weave doing what he could not, which was to face her,
that they might face each other, throats glistening
with stillness, again splendid temptation, voltage
upon voltage leaping in her blood—and before
she could say it, sweetheart, she stopped.

The Hen

This hen in my hands, a cold stream
pouring over it like over milky quartz,
this hunk of heavy hen, dead as stone.

You should've seen me driving home,
its corpse swaddled in a plastic sack
sprouting garlic and lemon-grass.

I did not stray from the road, though
I day-dreamed, greedy—whiff
of a roasted future curling

toward me, and my mouth watered.
It sat in the backseat, no longer hungry.
I had no reason to think about its life

until pieces dropped when I held it up:
gizzard and neck, its heart in the insinkerator.
Magnificent machine that did this, gutting

from the bird what's useless for this cook,
but bundles them back to remind him:
here are its gears, heart extinguished

down a dark hole. (I don't want to imagine
the hen in its row cage, clucking.) I wash
its cavity, spacious as a room for rent.

So surprising to be this intimate, to touch
its thighs, the folds of where its neck was—
a beautiful hen on its back

on the butcher block, hen who turns to me
as I rub its rafter ribs with salt, says, please,
Antonio, this will be you, be gentle.

Bamiyan

Because I wasn't there, I couldn't guess
what birds there would have been
that time of year, before the migrations.

If I could've glimpsed would they have
turned into sprung bough and dust,
retreat with the throngs to safer distance?

Suddenly the world appears to be made
of wind and extinction, and the wind dies.
I wasn't there, didn't feel the tremor

threading from bone to bone once the gods
were abandoned—And yet the broadcasted
ochres were magnificent; velvet shadows rose

out of smoke as if to persuade the orchards
somehow they must flower. The ground's
now covered with shards of an expression:

an eyelid's nook, nostrils without a scent
in them. When there's nothing left to praise,
praise how light scrambles into the rift

between you and I and softens the howling
of the jets; praise the quietude whose echoes
make it seem we are speaking to each other

across chasms. One day the hurt will be over.
I won't see you in the stones, and soot
will cease to remind me, but leaves only,

green to the heart. Once morning swells,
its tidy hours will cross the lawn,
unburdening each thing of its shadow,

and I shall know it plainly: I was looking
at a human body; that was why
the sunlight on the ground was broken.

Early Morning under Persimmon

Am the shape posed by the snow-
white percale, and under it's his body
being abolished in plain sight. He sleeps
like a heap of kindling which daylight
burns to no effect: nothing disturbs
the stillness of the sick or changes the terms.
What can make the bones go back to life,
the man to his wife speaking to her saints
in the chapel? Candlelight falls on bad times:
no longer can he come to her even as dust
carried by the most careless wind that wants
to remove her blouse. All day I watch this,
the pace of this and hear the ringing
solitude, the sound dreadful seconds make
when they have nowhere else to go.

No delay along the ladders of heather
and its lavender detonations. Each bee
saying to the flower's ear, I am not the hand
descending to pluck you. Trees all around
were leafed with starlings, and in my bewilderment,
I could not see a single source of the shrieks.
This could have been the Inferno, the wood
where if I snapped a branch it would cry out,
dark with blood and speak—a soul wounded
and glimpsed in poetry. I thought about
these bees sniffing for the powdery essence
in the heather—Whatever they found they still
couldn't tell me if the depths were transitive,
if the last steps were pallid as dry grass, or
suffused with expectation, honey for the sting.

The night is, the dew is, hours with no one
but rabbits, their backs flashing in the grass.
They flee hearing what wishes they'd freeze
in the middle of the moon's gaze, moon
so far it's useless to talk about distance.
When he lay down at noon I knew there'd be
no morning. If there were signs, I direct you
to the grass whose green supplanted the pool's
intensity as though rain had been falling
through the hours without disclosing its presence;
a bird would not leave the sill, sparrow which
found a home near the lord's altar, but no lord
was visible; the dog ran in circles as each of us
whispered into an ear of air, to the imperceptible
sacred heart, to the mask, the oxygen.

Though I knew it could not last I hung on to it
like an addiction—was secretly full of pleas
as they propped you up, flipped you over,
laid your body low after a kiss. Our goodnights
had been a loss: you were never the man again,
always reaching for what once resembled—
Did your eye ever deploy its imagination
to flush out what used to be recognizable,
a cheek, mouth now like a crater? At the end
the quiet deepened without attack, the inhalations
turned toward a calm that held no more surprise
and was not so terrible: his hands peacefully
opened to receive the hours that were filled
with shapes—a nurse, a wife beside,
a space where a son was supposed to be.

Morning. An explosion: it's the sprinklers.
The news opens its jaw and my head dips
into the text of the day—Turn the page:
the fire's burned out, and I will glean the fruit
from under the persimmon, like a hero,
and I will eat but cannot share, not least
with Dante who walks among the lost
in his poetry. On our knees we try to eliminate
the history, scrubbing pitched to the deepest
registers of memory. Foamy water spreads
its calm now that the dreadful's done:
the body burned, bedding and clothes.
No traffic, no barking dog, only dead road;
no one but us amid the hours and hours,
counting you among the missing.

Who can forget when the sky was vacant,
no jets but the black backs, black breasts
wheeling out of trees as if to chase the Trojans
with sad foretelling? A pair of tail-lights.
A tossed can of beer joins the lush haikus
of crickets as the cells labor toward their
full weights, bending the branch. Even the worm
pursues its design that begins with a wound
bitter to the bite, and still I swallow it.
Your hand will not climb to that which
you'd like to hold; you are insubstantial.
Constellations radiate through your shoulders,
cobwebs billow where you stood as dew
amplifies on fruit after fruit after fruit
that come to us from beyond destruction.

Crèvecoeur

Married to the task now, hanging the bells
on a thousand branches weighed down
with ripening gold, and the whole garden
watches: all birds, cats in the greedy bushes,
the oak punishing the grass with shade—
we're down to the dirt here, the stones.
Nothing exists but what has its enemy:
the poor fruit, all they can do is be beautiful,
wait for the bells to save them when who
or what alights, beak or hand, but only
one of us is frightened. Before this
there were so many blackbirds and the fruit
dropped to the street, all pierced, sweet ooze
out of the gaps. I picked up stones
under the rapid wings fleeing, threw:
one taken down. It lay in my gutter,
shattered wing without sound, the beak
dripping with persimmon. In the history
a farmer opened the pest like a chest
and found the bees it was devouring—
the crushed, the swallowed-whole still
pollen-heavy, golden fingers in the craw.
Nothing exists but what has its enemy:
he arranged the bees on a cloth, summer
sunshine helix felled there and there
as he counted them out like pebbles.

It was down to the bird and me, feeling
its heart thrash through windy feathers.
The mouth gurgled with persimmon
and persimmon, whereas some bees
(to his great surprise) returned to life,
then back to the hive. Here the bird spits,
the fruit sputtered, dappled the grass
when I thought to look at the grass.
I wish I were a god so that the bird,
the fruit—what use is wishing?
I can say: "This tree is beautiful,
these persimmons sweet," but the hand
gathering the dead and the ripe is my own.

Train to Agra

I want to reach you—
in that city where the snow

only shimmers silver
for a few hours. It has taken

seventeen years. This trip,
these characters patterned

in black ink, curves catching
on the page like hinges,

this weave of letters fraying
like the lines on my palm,

all broken paths. Outside,
no snow. Just the slow pull

of brown on the hills, umber
dulling to a bruise until the city

is just a memory of stained teeth,
the burn of white marble

to dusk, cows standing
on the edges like a dust

cloud gaining weight
after days of no rain. Asleep

in the hot berth, my parents
sway in a dance, the silence

broken by scrape of tin, hiss
of tea and underneath,

the constant clatter of wheels
beating steel tracks over and over

to the city of white marble,
to the city of goats, tobacco

fields, city of dead hands,
a mantra of my grandmother's—

her teeth eaten away
by betel leaves. The story

of how Shah Jahan had cut off
all the workers' hands

after they built the Taj, so they
could never build again. I dreamt

of those hands for weeks before
the trip, weeks even before I

stepped off the plane, thousands
of useless dead flowers drying

to sienna, silent in their fall.
Every night, days before, I dreamt

those hands climbing over the iron
gate of my grandparents' house, over

grate and spikes, some caught
in the groove between its sharpened

teeth, others biting where
they pinched my skin.

Spell

    for Lori

I thought it was the city, the muddled city.
Outside the car window—everything surging—

children scratching glass, never having seen anyone so pale,
broken animals, roads bitten away. India. When I look back

I will remember you crying in the heat of the car,
before we ever reached the Taj, before we climbed up

the steps, hot grass then cool marble under our feet. We thought
we had seen everything—the President's house, India Gate with its
    guards

and faded postcards, Quitar Minar where the man pulled
your arms behind your back, around the pillar for good luck.

You hoped it was worth the ache in your back that followed.
We traveled the city like we didn't belong, a place I should call home

but as foreign to me as to you. And you? Who can say why you cried,
two miles from the Taj in the city proper. My aunt thought it was the
    heat.

Maybe it was roaming the cluttered streets, no face your own,
or that smell when we stepped off the plane—

mixture of petroleum, spice and dust. Or was it dusk?
Then there were the stares, the calls to come look,

glass bangles shaken at us like charms, like some spell
and it was, with garlands stringing the runway like tiny beads of blood.

The India of Postcards

We began in one corner of the city
and plowed through cows and dung
and scooters, marbled and dusted
streets to the other. We were high
on heat and medicine. Anything
to protect our ourselves from disease,
and there were so many—cholera, malaria,
meningitis. All sounding soft and beautiful
on our lips, full of vowels and danger.
The only thing we wanted we couldn't have:
Water—unbottled, un-boiled—pure, sweet,
American-tasting water. With every sip,
a prayer to one of the gods: the god of good
health and an easy flight home, the god of
treasures hidden away in crowded street stalls.
There were other things, of course—trinkets
made of colored glass, hand-painted boxes, raw
silk—anything to say we had been there. Something
to hang on the walls of our tiny apartments. We were
looking for the gods, for the one thing
that shimmered more than silver, a pyramid
or temple, a country—something we couldn't fit
into our pockets. We wanted the India of postcards
with our faces on the front. Under all that glitter,
we wanted the shards of something we can't name.

Two Women

We squat in the cool grass gnawing
sugar cane. Brackish water brushes

the soles of our feet—your hair smells
of cloves, skin the color of sandalwood.

We talk of our men lost
in wars, lost in other women,

and of the children we gained:
sons, grandsons, daughters.

The sahib's wife calls, the green shutters
are open and Verdi drifts

in the air around us.
It is time to shake out

the dust-clogged rug,
clean the brandy glasses,

and feed the remains
to the waiting dogs.

Alignment

In Hindi, love is always the long version:
"you are in my heart." In Hindi movies,
you can tell it's a love scene because the man
and woman never kiss, just sing and gyrate
their hips towards each other. Love is splashed
like billboards all along the Delhi streets in a blur
of reds and blues.

*   *   *

Every time my grandmother tried to learn how
to drive, she got pregnant. She never learned
how to shift gears but she had three children.

*   *   *

I know the lines give me away. My palms hold
all the stories: you will lose like your mother
and great-grandmother, like all the women
in your family, all of them widows.

*   *   *

My grandmother at thirteen: married a man
she had never seen before the wedding day,
before the fire and the pundit. Fifty years
later, my grandmother at sixty-three:
"that was not the best way, but the only way."

*   *   *

Before the wedding, before years of marriage,
my parents consulted an astrologer to see
if their stars were aligned. Thirty years
of marriage based on stardust and heat.
Love is all numbers. The math insists upon it.

Suji Kwock Kim

The Couple Next Door

tend their yard every weekend,
when they paint or straighten
the purple fencepickets canting
each other at the edge of their lot,

hammering them down into soil
to stand. How long will they stay
put? My neighbors mend their gate,
hinges rusted to blood-colored dust,

then weave gold party-lights with
orange lobster-nets & blue buoys
along the planks. So much to see
& not see again, each chore undone

before they know it. I love how
faithfully they work their garden
all year, scumbling dried eelgrass
in fall, raking away mulch in spring.

Today the older one, Pat, plants
weeds ripped from a cranberry-bog.
Sassafras & pickerel, black locust
& meadowsweet, wild sarsaparilla,

checkerberry, starflower. Will they
take root here? Meanwhile Chris waters
seeds sown months ago. Furrows
of kale, snap-bean, scallion break

the surface, greedy for life. Muskrose
& lilac cast their last shadows. Is it
seeing or sun that makes them flicker,
as if they've vanished? They shake

like a letter in someone's hand.
Here come the guys from Whorfs
("Whores") Court, walking their dog
—also in drag—to the dunes.

I miss seeing Disorient Express
(a.k.a. Cheng, out of drag) walk by,
in tulle & sequins the exact shade
of bok choi. He must have endured

things no one can name, to name only
KS, pneumocystis, aplastic anemia.
I remember he walked off his gurney
when the ambulance came, then broke

his nurse's fingers in the hospital
when he tried to change his IV line,
wanting to live without meds. Zorivax,
Ativan, leucovorin? I don't know.

Pat & Chris pack down the loose dirt.
I'll never know what threads hold
our lives together. They kiss, then fall
on the grass. I should look away but don't.

Hanji: Notes for a Paper-Maker

for Liu Yoon-Young

Shaped like a slab of granite
marking a grave, but light,
airy as "spirit-sheaves" lashed
from bloodroot or star-thistle,

this sheet is not for burial
but making and making of:
a broth of splinters boiled to pith,
cast then clotted to blank.

I touch it, feeling grit and slub
silk, rough as braille. Is it
enough, is this how you hoped
to earn a living, making absence

palpable as pulp, though you laugh,
seeing I'm shocked at how much work
it took. Sow and mulch mulberry.
Slash the trunks down a year later—

chopping slant to sun so stumps
regrow—when their wood's still
tender but strong enough to keep,
no worms gnawing fleam or burl.

Soak, hack the black bark off,
tilt your knife at a sharp angle
to shave the green underskin
without cutting away good grain.

Scald the peeled rods with cotton-ash
so acid softens gnurl and knot.
Pound for hours until they're ground
to shreds, skeins of unlikely thread.

You show me your blistered hands.
Poor hands. When you strike a match
to fire, I almost feel the skin sting,
kerosene flaming *yontan*-coal.

I don't know what it costs you to love
this work. More than sulfur fumes
tasting of slag, flintsparks cracking,
engine-shunt as your cauldron simmers

hollyhock root to solder all
the elements in a strange solution,
an ecstasy, flecks shapeshifting,
hissing milk, spit, quicksilver.

While it smolders you drag
slung mold and bamboo-grill,
sieving with steady arms, long strokes
so fiber won't snarl at the heart.

You wring water, strip your grid,
letting grume clot to the hue
of skull-rot. It'll bleach in sun
to snow, tusk-tallow, peroxide—

depending how long it's left out,
on weather—or you'll dye it
with beets, indigo, sweet potato,
all the colors you have in mind.

In my mind you've become stern.
"For what you want to be, nothing
is something from another slant,
a slate, a plot to engrave spirit

in flesh, mirror or window or O.
Now you know how hard the labor is.
If your words aren't worth
my work, keep your mouth shut."

Monologue for an Onion

I don't mean to make you cry.
I mean nothing, but this has not kept you
From peeling away my body, layer by layer,

The tears clouding your eyes as the table fills
With husks, cut flesh, all the debris of pursuit.
Poor deluded human: you seek my heart.

Hunt all you want. Beneath each skin of mine
Lies another skin: I am pure onion—pure union
Of outside and in, surface and secret core.

Look at you, chopping and weeping. Idiot.
Is this the way you go through life, your mind
A stopless knife, driven by your fantasy of truth,

Of lasting union—slashing away skin after skin
From things, ruin and tears your only signs
Of progress? Enough is enough.

You must not grieve that the world is glimpsed
Through veils. How else can it be seen?
How will you rip away the veil of the eye, the veil

That you are, you who want to grasp the heart
Of things, hungry to know where meaning
Lies. Taste what you hold in your hands: onion juice,

Yellow peels, my stinging shreds. You are the one
In pieces. Whatever you meant to love, in meaning to
You changed yourself: you are not who you are,

Your soul cut moment to moment by a blade
Of fresh desire, the ground sown with abandoned skins.
And at your inmost circle, what? A core that is

Not one. Poor fool, you are divided at the heart,
Lost in its maze of chambers, blood, and love,
A heart that will one day beat you to death.

Montage with Neon, Bok Choi, Gasoline, Lovers & Strangers

None of the streets here has a name,
but if I'm lost
tonight I'm happy to be lost.

Ten million lanterns light the Seoul avenues
for Buddha's Birthday,
ten million red blue green silver gold moons

burning far as the eye can see in every direction
& beyond,
"one for every spirit,"
voltage sizzling socket to socket
as thought does,
firing & firing the soul.

Lashed by wind, flying up like helium balloons
or hanging still
depending on weather,

they turn each road into an earthly River of Heaven
doubling & reversing
the river above,

though not made of much:
some colored paper, glue, a few wires,
a constellation of poor facts.

I can't help feeling giddy.
I'm drunk on neon, drunk on air,
drunk on seeing what was made

almost from nothing: if anything's here at all
it was built
out of ash, out of the skull-rubble of war,

the city rising brick by brick
like a shared dream,
every bridge & pylon & girder & spar a miracle,

when half a century ago
there was nothing
but shrapnel, broken mortar-casings, corpses,

the War Memorial in Itaewon counting
MORE THAN 3 MILLION DEAD, OR MISSING—
still missed by the living, still loved beyond reason,

monument to the fact
that no one can hurt you, no one kill you
like your own people.

I'll never understand it.
I wonder about others I see on the sidewalks,
each soul fathomless—

strikers & scabs walking through Kwanghwamoon,
or "Gate of Transformation by Light,"
riot police rapping nightsticks against plexiglass-shields,

hawkers haggling over cell phones or silk shirts,
shaking dirt from *chamae* & bok choi,
chanting price after price,

fishermen cleaning tubs of cuttlefish & squid,
stripping copper carp,
lifting eels or green turtles dripping from tanks,

hanyak peddlars calling out names of cures
for sickness or love—
crushed bees, snake bile, ground deer antler, chrysanthemum root,

bus drivers hurtling past in a blast of diesel-fumes,
lovers so tender with each other
I hold my breath,

dispatchers shouting the names of stations,
the grocer who calls me "daughter" because I look like her,
for she has long since left home,

vendors setting up *pojangmachas*
to cook charred silkworms, broiled sparrows,
frying sesame-leaves & mung-bean pancakes,

men with hair the color of scallion root
playing paduk, or GO,
old enough to have stolen overcoats & shoes from corpses,

whose spirits could not be broken,
whose every breath seems to say:
after things turned to their worst, we began again,

but may you never go through what we went through,
may you never see what we saw,
may you never remember & may you never forget.

Coup de Grâce

Bodies made solid by weights succumb
to illness. Years of focused practice

lost in that afternoon of neglect.
What we are felt after the fact—

walls with his name graffitied on them,
late night actors who could've been

his double. Dolls left in a drawer
unopened for years like those boxes

of books in the attic that became
our inheritance. The things loved least

loved at last. Weather vanes renewed
by wind. But the former tenants are gone.

Our words a bridge. Just as my kiss
once sealed the tomb of his empty mouth.

An Evening Train

whistles past hacked-down fields of corn,
heading towards a boy who whittles
an effigy of himself. We go on sleeping
through sirens and crimson strobes
that flash on remains no one can identify
till we line up at dawn to see who's
missing. At the zoo this morning, a girl
found half-devoured in a moat, two lions
licking their chops, *Little Rock, Arkansas*
the only proof left on her body to show
how far she was from home. A tattered copy
of *The Odyssey* later found in her purse.
Did she love her life? We warn our children
not to lay their heads down on the tracks
in wintertime, knowing how it's not
always best to know what's coming our way.

The Assignation

Overshadowed by the sound of a beak
scraping cuttlebone, smell of sperm

in that room where crushed saltines
were whistled out of open mouths—

a mermaid carved into the headboard
of an antique bed still whispering

to that married man who had not yet
made up his mind. Were we ever able

to inhabit the paradise hour replete
with kisses steeped in votive wine?

Never seem strong enough to tear up
the letters while birds flew overhead—

bodies pushed through zones of cold
as we dove down deeper into the river.

Winter

Stalks of hacked-down corn poking through snow.

Wanting to replace or be replaced he said.

Bullets in slow-motion mapping the hunter's arc.

Where the compass fell a sign of distress.

A school of swollen tongues darting at his balls.

Frozen waterfalls embroidered onto silk.

Lodged inside his throat by the edge of the road.

Monologue with the Void

Your face to be erased. Your file

deleted. This at century's end—

not Charing Cross Road where people

met. No kewpie dolls. Mack trucks

highjacked where he-men stop to take

a leak. The dog days of August

where one can never drink too much!

An ocean between us. Like skin

to bone, your smile a rictus, cock

sliding up my crack somewhere in

cyberspace. Me no longer able

to sleep—unread messages from here

to what we would call a virtual

loss. New epic. Till lovers log off.

Warren Liu

Li Po Declines

After the rain the windows reply dimension,
> *Since I was called, I came, through history's vapor and steel,*

echoed back four times in cars passing soundlessly.
> *but here, am not liable to answer how the moonlight 'quavers'*

Beyond the window's window I am set, quadrangled,
> *on the river. My love has no slippered feet of ivory,*

poetically asking of the poet Li Po
> *my wars are dripped from cask to mouth only.*

tell me friend, is it true, *in vino veritas?*
> *These orchards are not weeping in their ripeness. If my head is*
> *bowed low*

What whisper tickles the ear of your wine jug?
> *it is only mimicry, only respectfully feigned sleep.*

After the rain, tell me, why do the streetcars
> *Since I was called through the folds of bossy imagination I came*

stretch toward me a proffered line, as a hand?
> *powdered in lotus flowers, fragrantly ominous*

Though the streets bespeak no secret.
> *or serene. Likewise my head is a giant peach, faint pink tumor*

There is no soundtrack to this walking, wet and heavy,
> *of wisdom, you may touch it but please don't bump.*

no trumpets of arrival to this bar, curtained
I cannot answer your rainy questions, invader, but insist we share

with smoke, beyond which, layers of fuzz, of dropsy.
a glass of fire-water and compare birdsongs, lute to lute.

After the wet and heavy even the roads divided
Since I was called, I must remind you,

are divided by guitar strings, my head twanging
and it would do you well to remember this next time,

without me towards a tinier vibration,
the folds in my robe are real, but tenuous. I am not from the same place

while the faithless transit nestles deeply in its tracks.
you are not from.

El Niño

I took hold of a hand that was slippery to melting.

The night closed around me like fleshy jaws. I wanted to sing
but the air was rhythmless,

the ground covered with miniature frogs.

The sky stamping down like giant's feet.

I ran with the scissors pointing skywards,
yelling "unfair! unfair!"

But being chased is not as hilarious as chasing.

*

Later, the tea was too hot in its white milkiness,
i.e. the quavering legs of the table.

There was strange dialogue between the dripping ceiling
and your wet eyelashes.
Pipes overhead rumbled, washed-out, obligatory.

A radio-control car with car-bomb zoomed between my feet,
an action figure poised on the hood shouting
"unfair! unfair!," i.e. a salute.

Surely the night was fallacy: *escargot, zinfandel, darjeeling,
flan.* I was leaking i.e. mentally.

Because it all blended into a disturbing appropriateness,
upright with disarming regularity.

*

Actually, I found myself surrounded by houses
of a uniform shit color.
Summer was a heaviness of air: opening around me,
doors of water: a gummy hammock.
I lay in it half wanting, half not.

Often the streets were overrun with variations of nothing.
At night, D. ran stomping in imitation
of the Abominable Snowman—underfoot the snails
covered the street, a layer of eggshells arranged
as if only that once, the Gods favored the Sadists.

What I said before? Disregard that.

*

El Cerrito, then. In a house that spewed its sewage
onto the front lawn.

Our hands met in secret conversation in my pocket,
inside the fire—inside, the fire

was turning shades of green and burgundy. *Burgundy,* I said.
Hurdy-gurdy, you said.

Another voice said, *Solomon Grundy.*

Which explains the command given me by the wind:

For that which is not fair is not fair to all?
For that which is not unfair is not unfair by default.

*

Which explains the command given me by the night:
You shall not drink *Burgundy* until you kneel in ecstatic
discharge. Forsake not the porcelain.

Friends and lovers will lower their heads as you pass by.
They will snicker as they call you *El Presidente.*

You will look for the wind of that night as a sorrowless man
looks for sorrow:

not *through* it but *in* it.

"Be You Ever So Lonesome"

He wanted the woman in the room—or at least the woman's head seen
through the window from where he sat, which wasn't nearly close
enough to see more than her head bobbing upon the lower frame of the
window, as if strung by a rope from the ceiling—he wanted her to turn
toward him, sitting so far away and outside. He knew that it was close to
the time when she would go to bed, the head would soon disappear
from view and the lights go off. She seemed to have black or very dark
brown hair, a bob it's called, correct, since her head bobs, she's wearing
a bob. Certainly her name is not Bob, but perhaps Bobbie. The light
three windows up, two windows over flashes on and then off, on, and
then off again, what's that, he wonders, a mistake or code? *smells
nothing like strawberries* Not for him since it's barely possible anyone in
the building at any point along the x or y axis of windows could see him
sitting there out on the steps of the dark stairway, but maybe she could?
yikes! what is he doing down there And then again what if she were to

turn her head enough so that he could match the profile to the portrait? There are certain patterns for instance when the light from window x4 y6 goes on the light from x3 y7 goes off, almost every night, *rat fink motherfucker* he imagines the two are linked, linked for years driving insane the two occupants of, let's see 1st floor 100 so 6th floor 600, seventh 700, correct, so perhaps occupant 610 and occupant 705, *james those pants couldn't possibly be any uglier* out of his mind angina-bound because for some reason every night precisely at 11 pm—or thereabouts—his light goes off, just as he's getting ready to embark on the crossword or maybe it's a she, *someone who was entirely the victim of ideological delusion would not even be able to recognize an emancipatory claim upon them, ugh* she's finishing the sweater for her godson, one last stitch. Likewise 610 cannot understand why her light decides to switch on every night at 5 am just as she's approaching the last hurdle, poised upon Ivy, the horse she rides in her dream, *ample time for a quick stroll, perhaps bourbon?* what's the name for that sport he asks no-one in particular. *atop Ivy, an equestrienne* The newish couple never shutters the blinds, exhibitionists maybe, though never naked, he wishes they were, at least one anyhow, because from so far away and outside it's impossible to tell if it's a man and a woman, or a woman and a woman, or a woman and a man, which is different than a man and a woman, in subtle and confounding ways, correct. They are often in the kitchen cooking, and he knows somehow with absolute certitude, can even sometimes hear the popping grease, it's sausages. Sausages, he thinks, are disgusting. They never feed each other, and one is often eating an apple.

Ravine

as they come
through the endless branchings of rooms
after bronze Chinese coins are cast
strange heat of silences
you stand doused in sleep

the back of your neck
is a bird's shadow ascending
your spine a line
a ravine where things are lost:
marbles   the sound of a cello
faded photos   brittle letters
I lace your body with my hands
your legs   loaves of bread
your feet   slippery fish
broken fins
swimming through uncharted waters

under your right shoulder blade
I find something shiny   black
a new revolver

as they come for you
I wipe sleep off your shoulders
put the gun in your hands
tell you to aim
you point
to your head

Field

Crows land like horses' neighs
rush of rocks

how many buffaloes
does it take to plow a disaster?
how many women to clean
up the mess?

shoots of incense
hotly in her hands
she bows towards the tombstones
face of her son
how many revolutions for us to realize?

her windless grey hair
becomes her   she knows this
there is no reason
to dye what she's earned

rain quiet as wings
on her back

Letters

She has become like her mother
her insides blooming
she calms the gusts of hands & feet
heartbeats delicate as geranium buds

he's the salve of her sleep
                    writing her letters over eleven years
before the rats nibble on them
                                        the house reads the words of his
    delirium
        which keeps the beams from rotting
                    the cracks from spreading paint from fading
                        blanketing sun & moon the mist
        grays the decade

    at times he shakes from malaria
                forehead feverish   ice in his bones
                    salve of his
                disease she's eleven years away

    her one eye
                observes the grapefruit rinds worming
                        on the dirt
        a love letter seen askew
    divides the days of mist
                    the house too having read
                            them is preserved

Emerald World

1
        i stopped trying to make sense of the scenes:
    the schizophrenic watching tv 12 hours a day
                                the alcoholic with eyes of red ants
                    the hotel manager   his chicken-meat dripping blood
                a hand floating   the Serbs killing
sun jumps off window   plummets to ground
        wild ducks break the mirror

2

a melancholy Vietnamese song whimpers
                        its syllables like porcelain bowls

3

    i remember the future
as seagulls tumble from slit in stratus clouds

                men walk with eyes grown onto their buttocks
                                others have stomachs flat to
    sand
                a woman   breasts dangling white & vocal
        the ocean's octave heard
                crashing

                        against breakwaters
            heard so often it isn't

4

    under the sea's umbrage
                    touching everything in sight
        density springs
                        from light & the elements
nothing less but the world at stake

5

                            i remember
            the future   that i'm fated to something odd
        to have patience the color of a refrigerator
                            synchronicity &
            a forest of emerald Buddhas

Overhearing Water

                                        ears pressed i listen
                        the drowsy delta
                                sea-salt deep in my nostrils

        used for the morning & evening meals
                                    water   pumped from the sewage the streets

                                                    rush down legs
                    & alleyways (rooms wet from thought)
                                            clink against
                        sodden sidewalks odored
                                with my hair as i wash upon rising
                        clothes washed scrubbed
                sound of tubs
                        agreeing in the sudsy hands
                of a woman her willful children about her

        i want to dream but i hear
                            women pailing men pumping
                                                ion luring ion
                            electron repulsing electron gurgling
                            feet always wet faces hands

                winter comes
                        we wash in the cold
                    in doused nights
                                seasick the straw mat a cat tramples at midnight
    i want to breathe but what breath

        a woman still washes her husband's & daughter's clothes
                                    wringing the clothes hushed

between life & death
                                    i hear poured into round tubs
            emptied choke
                        of water   tub against concrete
    the woman rinses her hands & feet

            between day & night
                                    sounds of gravity
            at 5:30 the first person wakes
        to rinse her phlegm mouth
            noise of work begins
                                with an avalanche of insomnia
                    morning drunkenness slippers
    & mothers prodding their children to school   i see the wash of smoke & tv
        ash   radio
                                            music bellowing
            the seventies the eighties Brothers in Arms
                        a dusky voice like a flower hanging
    & the girl downstairs begins to wash her endless
                    ebony hair

        the walkway leading to the 22 families' houses
                                rivulets roving
            down roof
        concrete algae-green

        all overhearing water
                    Haø Noäi's innards alchemize to jade

Aimee Nezhukumatathil

Fishbone

At dinner, my mother says if one gets stuck
in your throat, roll some rice into a ball
and swallow it whole. She says things
like this and the next thing out of her mouth

is *did you know Madonna is pregnant?*
But I want to ponder the basket of fried smelt
on the table, lined with paper towels to catch
the grease—want to study their eyes

like flat soda, wonder how I'm supposed
to eat them whole. Wonder why we can't
have normal food for breakfast like at Sara's house—
Cheerios, or sometimes if her mother is home:

buttered toast and soft-boiled eggs
in her grandmother's dainty blue egg cups
and matching blue spoon. Safe. Pretty.
Nothing with eyes. Under the flakes of fried crust,

I see a shimmer of skin as silver as foil,
like the dimes my mother tapes to a board
for each year I'm alive. How she tucked this
into my suitcase before I left for college

and I forgot about '93 *and* '95. How she said
she'll never find a '93, and shouldn't this
be a great thing to one day put into an oak frame,
but not now, not until we find the missing coin?

How we don't have many traditions left, thanks
to Your Father. These are the things she says
instead of a blessing to our food. These are the words
that stick inside me as I snap off the next head.

A Date with a Cherry Farmer

Of course I regret it. I mean there I was under umbrellas of fruit
so red they *had* to be borne of Summer, and no other season.
Flip-flops and fishhooks. Ice cubes made of lemonade and sprigs
of mint to slip in blue glasses of tea. I was dusty, my ponytail
all askew and the tips of my fingers ran, of course, *red*

from the fruitwounds of cherries I plunked into my bucket
and still—he must have seen some small bit of loveliness
in walking his orchard with me. He pointed out which trees
were sweetest, which ones bore double seeds—puffing out
the flesh and oh the surprise on your tongue with two tiny stones

(a twin spit), making a small gun of your mouth. Did I mention
my favorite color is red? His jeans were worn and twisty
around the tops of his boot; his hands thick but careful,
nimble enough to pull fruit from his trees without tearing
the thin skin; the cherry dust and fingerprints on his eyeglasses.

I just know when he stuffed his hands in his pockets, said
Okay. Couldn't hurt to try? and shuffled back to his roadside stand
to arrange his jelly jars and stacks of buckets, I had made
a terrible mistake. I just know my summer would've been
full of pies, tartlets, turnovers—so much jubilee.

Mouth Stories

> "Its ridges, valleys, the corrugated roof, the fortress of teeth.
> There's a story trapped inside my mouth."
> —Jeanette Winterson's *Written on the Body*

sweet

Tight places between the molars,
the hollow under the tongue—
syrup-thick with desire, I find
my favorite place on your chest.
Your lips parted small while you sleep:
banana ice cream kiss.

sour

I leave your house before you
wake. The smash-smash of dead
leaves crumbles from the dark
corners of your frown. The ink
on yesterday's paper, cover
from the rain, drools down my cheek.

bitter

Like unripened pears for breakfast,
nausea rises into the back of my throat
when I think of your breath
warming someone else's thigh—
bottom lip cracked cold, I swallow
the last bit of blood.

salty

The skin between your shoulder
and neck is fresh on my tongue.
The first tear from your Bohemian
blue eye I lapped up by chance,
the second on purpose; I cannot rid
this taste from my mouth.

What I Learned from the Incredible Hulk

When it comes to clothes, make
an allowance for the unexpected.
Be sure the spare in the trunk
of your station wagon with wood paneling

isn't in need of repair. A simple jean jacket
says *Hey, if you aren't trying to smuggle*
rare Incan coins through this peaceful
little town and kidnap the local orphan,

I can be one heck of a mellow kinda guy.
But no matter how angry a man gets, a smile
and a soft stroke on his bicep can work
wonders. I learned that male chests

also have nipples, warm and established—
green doesn't always mean envy.
It's the meadows full of clover
and chicory the Hulk seeks for rest, a return

to normal. And sometimes, a woman
gets to go with him, her tiny hands
correcting his rumpled hair, the cuts
in his hand. Green is the space between

water and sun, cover for a quiet man,
each rib shuttling drops of liquid light.

Red Ghazal

I've noticed after a few sips of tea, the tip of her tongue, thin and red
with heat, quickens when she describes her cuts and bruises—deep
    violets and red.

The little girl I baby-sit, hair orange and wild, sits splayed and upside
    down
on a couch, insists her giant book of dinosaurs is the only one she'll ever
    read.

The night before I left him, I could not sleep, my eyes fixed on the
    freckles
of his shoulder, the glow of the clock, my chest heavy with dread.

Scientists say they'll force a rabbit to a bird, a jellyfish with a snake, even
though the pairs clearly do not mix. Some things are not meant to be
    bred.

I almost forget the weight of a man sitting beside me in bedsheets
    crumpled
around our waists, both of us with magazines, laughing at the thing he
    just read.

He was so charming—pointed out planets, ghost galaxies, an ellipsis
of ants on the wall. And when he kissed me goodnight, my neck
    reddened.

I'm terrible at cards. Friends huddle in for Euchre, Hearts—beg me to
    play
with them. When it's obvious I can clearly win with a black card, I
    throw down a red.

I throw away my half-finished letters to him in my tiny pink
    wastebasket, but
my aim is no good. The floor is scattered with fire hazards, declarations
    unread.

The Shirt His Father Wore That Day Was Wrinkled, Slightly

It is a stunt
Kenji Takezo finds himself
Performing unexpectedly.
The rhythm of the Pacific in his feet,
He leaps
Onto the ironing board
His mother is getting ready
To straighten his father's
Work clothes, the creases
After a good washing.

Kenji takes a stance
Wide enough to support
His center of gravity,
Flexes his knees
Counterbalancing the instability
Of water, his arms
Apart for symmetry.

He watches
The crest of a wave
Pitch over and enclose him,
Hears in the chamber
The silent pulse of its heart.
As the walls close in,
Kenji crouches lower,
Leans forward to escape
The collapsing ocean.

The ironing table floats
The small boy
Only for a moment
Too much weight in front, it purls
Nose-first, into thick
Brown shag.
His mother, bringing the cold
Iron and a bundle of laundry,
Sees just in time
Kenji diving into the deep
Cushion of their couch.

When he surfaces,
Her expression is one
He has never seen
One that is completely new
To the muscles in her face.

Kenji has broken
Her favorite ironing table—
A wedding gift from the Yamaguchis.
The legs, split beyond
Their crotch.

His mother on her knees
Tries to iron on the ruined table
Anyway. His father needs
A shirt to impress
The same co-workers
He sees daily.
In this posture, his mother's movements
Remind Kenji of a surfer
Waxing the board she will ride.

From Rooftops, Kenji Takezo Throws Himself

Be Prepared—Boy Scout Motto

In midair, he hesitates at the moment
Gravity begins its pull. Before closing
His eyes, he peeks at the earth
Spinning below him, wonders why
When he jumps into space
The planet never abandons him.

The trick, he must remember, is in the landing:
Keep his face and genitals out of it.
Adjusting himself in the air,
He arches his back and bends
His flailing arms and legs behind,
A broken swan plunging from the ten-foot heavens.
When he smacks the cool cement
Belly first, his heart bounces. Still, he holds
The wind, usually, inside him.

A year ago the ocean rose
Six feet before it turned and collapsed.
Tackled firmly, he saw nothing but white.
His belly slapped the sand.
His breath knocked free. Ten minutes
He struggled, floating without
Weight, until it was recovered
Safely from the grip of water.

To be certain he never again fumbles
The breath he has kept since birth,
He rehearses the vertical flight
Every day, making his stomach strong.
Next week he will start
Leaping off two- and three-story buildings
Preparing for the wipeouts he will take
When he falls from waves
The size of cathedrals.

The Ocean Inside Him

After Kenji Takezo fell from a wave,
The turbulence of whitewash confused
His sense of direction.
He breathed in
When he should have

Held tight. By accident, he swallowed
The Pacific. The water poured down his throat,
A blue cascade he could not see.
He felt in his stomach
The heavy life of the ocean.

It wasn't funny, but he giggled
When a school of fish tickled his ribs.
He went home, the surf not rideable,
It was no longer there,
The water weighted in his belly.

That night, while he slept, the tide moved.
The long arms of the moon
Reached inside him pulling the Pacific free.
When he woke the next morning,
He lay in a puddle of ocean that was his.

With Her at All Times Ethel Nakano Carried a Sledgehammer

Everywhere she went, she swung the mallet with ease.
She never knew when she might need it.
At the supermarket, the bank, the autoclub, she kept
The tool nearby waiting for that exact moment
When a sledgehammer was necessary.
The occasions in which excessive pounding was required.
If a door needed to be forced open, Ethel Nakano was ready.
The instrument was a natural extension of her,
The long wood handle and solid iron head were a limb,
Another appendage, only very heavy on one end.

Ethel Nakano with her sledgehammer was endowed.
She was not at all large or burly, but well equipped she was
With centrifugal force behind her. She could wreck easily
A hairdryer or an oven, a stone wall or a car,
In just one, maybe two, exacting blows.
She had the strength of gravity and she used it skillfully.
One hand gripping the base of the handle, the other
Choked up near the throat, she lifted the mallet above
Her head, then let the weight drop down to find its target.
This talent for smashing took her years to cultivate.

When she walked through town with her tool in hand,
Ethel Nakano appeared much taller, more threatening
Than she really was. But people who knew her knew
She was not a dangerous person. She was just
A kind woman, a good citizen, who welcomed
The opportunity to give a solid whack, the chance to slam
Her sledgehammer against another object.
Indeed, Ethel Nakano was often too quick on the draw.
A mishap once occurred after she heard
That a neighborhood cat was trapped in a mailbox.

While there was no celebrated rescue that day,
The damage she did is a permanent reminder to all
That Ethel Nakano was capable of destruction.

A Man Made Himself a Marionette

His behavior at times was unmanageable.
Too often, Paul Tanaka lived by impulse
So that he found himself always

Performing acts that got him in trouble:
The time he danced in traffic
Leaping from car to car to cross the street,

Or the incident in which he climbed
A telephone pole to eat his lunch.
Paul Tanaka could not control these whims,

These urges to engage in folly.
He grew tired of himself doing
At the moment whatever beseeched him.

No more did he want to suffer
The unexpected aftermath of these occasions.
Somehow he separated enough of himself

From himself that he understood
He needed to monitor his actions.
So he fashioned strings to his hands,

His feet, his head to gain control.
The ends pulled behind his back were gathered
Into a main knot where he could manage

Himself. At first he had difficulty negotiating
His movements. But with practice
The strings inspired his reason.

Paul Tanaka became a master of commanding his own life.
Now, every motion was executed
Only after he considered all the consequences.

Soon he recognized that this was not a good thing.
He ruled, with absolute power, too much of himself
So that an itch took more than scratch.

Relieving an agitation inside his own skin was not
A simple response to which he directed his fingertips.
To avoid any unfortunate outcomes,

Paul Tanaka had to analyze all
The possible results of such a response.
But by thinking everything through so thoroughly,

The itch was lost, the inspiration disappeared.
He no longer wanted an authority to control his life
So he stretched for the strings to untie himself

But the main knot was just outside of his grasp.
Each time he extended his reach
The puppeteer hoisted it far and away from him.

Eventually he learned to resign himself,
The man who wished for a little discipline, to live
The life of a dummy.

Jon Pineda

Shelter

Have you forgotten the way my face winced at my father
when, instead of shaking your hand, he walked off sputtering
mestizo in a language I knew you didn't understand?
I have closed a small space of my heart, packed it
with jars of figs, canned tomatoes, blankets and jugs
of fresh water. We could open them, dip our fingers first
into the preserves and then into each other's mouth.
Inside these walls, under blankets, we could wait
for the storm.

Birthmark

After they make love, he slides down so his face rests near her waist. The
light by the bed casts its nets that turn into shadows. They fall asleep.
When he wakes, he finds a small patch of birthmarks on her thigh, runs
his finger over each island, a spec of light brown bundled with others to
form an archipelago on her skin. For him, whose father is from the
Philippines, it is the place he has never been, filled with hillsides of rice
and fish, different dialects, a family he wants to touch, though
something about it all is untouchable. Like love, balanced between
desire and longing, the way he reaches for her now, his hand pressed
near this place that seems so foreign, so much a part of him that, for a
moment, he feels whole.

Translation

We thought nothing of it, he says,
though some came so close
to where we slept.

I try to see him as a boy,
back in the Philippines, waking

to the sound of machine guns.
His family would spend their morning

spreading a paste over the sores
of the house's thick walls.

He tells how he touched
points where bullets entered,

his fingers, he says, *disappeared into the holes,*

as if inside there existed a space where everything
from this world could vanish.

Here we could place the memory of my sister,
his daughter, who died after a car wreck.

Wedge her into the smoky path
and cover her in sunlight.

The family next door is raking leaves in the yard.

A father scolds his children
for jumping into large piles
he arranged into a crescent moon.

We cannot hear them from inside,
but I feel they are frightened
as he grabs both of them
around the waist and spins.

I wait for the ending
to my father's story,
but he is too busy smiling,

as if enjoying the silence
of those bullets in concrete.

This Poetry

It is where she has gone. A spoon clicks
in her mouth while her eyes fall back.

And the one holding her hand is not me
or you. It is a boy, her brother, and he is afraid,

though he remembers something about pressing
a spoon to her tongue so that metal catches

the flesh, so that the tongue does not follow
the eyes into leaving a part of this world.

Years later, this boy will read he was wrong
for using a spoon. He will spend the summer

lifeguarding at a pool, and more than once, he will
hold a body while it seizes in waist-high water.

Each one returns the same way, a pause and then
their life, all they have ever known, rushing back

into the mind. Forget the boy in the beginning.
He has grown into someone who spends too much

time remembering. For this, he has already lost a part
of himself. And from those people he saved, holding

them in the sun as they came to, the color in their eyes
sharp as glass, there was a time when he thought

this could be her, a body becoming weightless.
Then a stranger cried in his arms. She didn't

know anyone around her, especially him.
It did not matter. This is not about remembering.

Forget there was ever a spoon. Forget the sound
metal makes against the teeth and the tongue.

Forget it all and come back to your life.

Losing a Memory

After watching a woman's fingers
sink into a loaf of bread
and scatter its pieces over a river,
I have tried to remember how water held part
of an evening sun, itself held back by a shadow
of spires on the hill, gently tapping along the Vltava
until swans disrupted the water.
It was almost communion, and yet this thought
of almost being *something* slowly passed
as the swans bundled together, diving one
after the other.

Earlier, I thought I saw her in the crowd
rising out of the metro stop at Staromestska,
her eyes opening the way each umbrella spread
beneath a light rain ending in the street.
It was only the way those strangers disappeared,
huddled and turning into alleyways, sound. A horn
made me realize I was standing too close to the curb.
The driver screamed in his language as he passed, shaking
his fist into a quietly subsiding fury.

I have forgotten or remembered.
Whenever I think of death, her absence
becomes a sheath of wings disappearing into a dark body
or a candle wick giving into its own weight
and slipping beneath a surface that will harden,
maybe to be re-lit tomorrow night, adding its light
to the shadowy room of a café where a woman reads
aloud from a book she has written, poem after poem,
about love.

Srikanth Reddy

Burial Practice

Then the pulse.
Then a pause.
Then twilight in a box.
Dusk underfoot.
Then generations.

*

Then the same war by a different name.
Wine splashing in a bucket.
The erection, the era.
Then exit Reason.
Then sadness without reason.
Then the removal of the ceiling by hand.

*

Then pages & pages of numbers.
Then the page with the faint green stain.
Then the page on which Prince Theodore, gravely wounded, is thrown
    onto a wagon.
Then the page on which Masha weds somebody else.
Then the page that turns to the story of somebody else.
Then the page scribbled in dactyls.
Then the page which begins *Exit Angel.*
Then the page wrapped around a dead fish.
Then the page where the serfs reach the ocean.
Then a nap.
Then the peg.
Then the page with the curious helmet.
Then the page on which millet is ground.
Then the death of Ursula.

Then the stone page they raised over her head.
Then the page made of grass which goes on.

*

Exit Beauty.

*

Then the page someone folded to mark her place.
Then the page on which nothing happens.
The page after this page.
Then the transcript.
Knocking within.

Interpretation, then harvest.

*

Exit Want.
Then a love story.

Then a trip to the ruins.
Then & only then the violet agenda.

Then hope without reason.
Then the construction of an underground passage between us.

Hotel Lullaby

No matter how often you knock
on the ocean the ocean

just waves. No matter
how often you enter the ocean

the ocean still says
no one's home. You must leave

her dear Ursula. As I write this
they polish the big

chandelier. Every prism
a sunset in abstract

or bijou foyer depending
on where you stand.

They take it apart every Fall
& call it Spring cleaning.

They bring me my tea.
They ask me my name

& I tell them—Ursula,
I don't even know

how to miss who you left.
So many cabanas

to choose from tonight
but only one view.

It's the sea.
What keeps me awake

is the sound of you sleeping
beside me again my dear Ursula,

Ursula dear—then
you're nothing
but waves & I break.

Circle (I)

It's dark in here, the dark inside of a man
in the dark. It's not night. One hears crows
overhead, dawn fowl caws, the shod soles again

treading their sunlit plots above. One grows
dotish-fond of these things. Long live the things,
their ways, their roots pushed goatish & grey

through the skull, in this earth that gaily spins
though one has crossed its smutted green threshold
to reign in a crate. We have done no wrong,

my friends, & yet we find ourselves soiled,
sold, carbonized teeth in a moss-riven jaw.
Once, I sat on a stool as my grandmother told

me of heaven, cleaning fish for our supper. I saw
her rust-flaked edge unseam the sunset
in each belly—coral, ochre, carmine, raw

lice-infested sunsets in a pail. So many nights.
Night in the kitchen shack, night at the crumbling edge
of our milk-pond province, a blade, lone cricket

raving in the lawn.

Circle (VI)

This is my latest recording. It is the sound of a man & a woman not speaking. The beauty of this silence lies in what you can hear when you turn up the volume. I have tried many times to capture this version of nothing, but women are few when one lives in this manner. Continual tears are the object. The reading of books is forbidden. Assuming an upright position is strictly forbidden. One's meals are hauled up in a bucket which can be used afterwards as a latrine & sent down again. In this manner, one's needs are satisfied. By pointing or performing simple gestures it is possible to communicate everything necessary to carry on living. A finger upraised is the firmament. The hand extended palm forward means blessing or stop.

Palinode

There is no Ursula, Ursula. Never was there any balcony braving the waves. Nothing was promised, no buttons undone. There's only this silence lit by a dangling bulb & some woman's cracked voice hissing Silence. I regret to inform you that there is no reason for tears. No horses were slain at Magenta. Birkenau was not named for birches. I should know, for I have inspected the documents for hours on end without making a sound. If you were to crawl to me across this great marble chamber with its hallways & crooked columns of volumes, I might reconsider. That would be reason for tears, but no Ursula crawls. No paramour whores herself under these trestles. When it gets lonely, I sit by the river & read. Correction. There is no river. Mostly, I read.

Stupid

> In Detroit, a 41-year-old gets stuck and drowns
> in two feet of water after squeezing his head through
> a narrow sewer grate to retrieve his car keys.

A joke? Tell me

the story of Job, that book of the pious man
who suffered because the devil wanted to teach God
faith kills through illusion. *Sub*
+ *ferrere* = to carry, to wear boils

like a string of pearls around the neck
and watch son, wealth, house turn
into a sootfall of ash. *Suffer*

the little children I thought was an imperative
not to love but to disdain.
Tell me the one about Santiago Alvarado
who died in Lompoc, having fallen

through the ceiling of the shop
he burgled when the flashlight he carried in his mouth
rammed into his skull.

How Nick Berrena was stabbed to death
by a friend trying to prove a knife couldn't penetrate
the flakvest Berrena wore,
or Daniel Jones dug an 8–foot hole in the sand
whose broad shelf buried him alive.

Hast not thou made an hedge

about him, and about all he hath on every side?
Skin for skin, yea, all that a man hath
he will give for his life.
Tell me what the foolish

should make with their small faith
in roofing, keys just a fingerhold away. This world,
shimmering with strange death in which we know
that to trip on the staircase, wreck the lover's car
is perhaps also to sit covered with ash eating
one's own white heart.

Why doesn't the universe turn a lovelier face to me?

A woman runs to a poison control center
after eating three vaginal inserts while a man
has a cordless phone pulled from his rectum.
I comfort friends

badly, curse the stove for my meal,
live with the wrong man for years. Faith
for me extends just as far as I'm rewarded; if I laugh
about the mouth foaming with nonoxynal
I'm also awed by the woman's belief propelling her *toward*
not *away from* fear, contrary to skepticism or evidence.

Are there not mockers with me?

And doth mine eye not continue in their provocation?
Bildad begged Job take the smarter path of self-blame:
the sinner must be punished with sin, the stupid destroyed
by stupidity. *Shall the earth be forsaken for thee?* he asked.

How long will ye mock me? Job cried. God waits
and his words blush furiously up to heaven.

Stupid. Job is stupid for believing.
And I am one of the false mockers chastising
endlessly the faith of one who suffers,
who produces no great thing but shame: to wait

is to destroy the organ and a rash act
must mar this soul. *Stupid,*
how can you love me when everything I give you hurts?

Satan is an old joke to us who don't know

how many temptations lurk
in the commonest household:
the knife, the flashlight. But Santiago knows

and if stealing is the thing that brings one closer
to happiness, and keeping one's hands
free means the difference
between this life and death, that's one line he'll cross.

Few people die intelligently,

the mind gone, shit or urine trickling
between sheets: why not be stabbed
believing yourself protected from the physical indignity
of a knife? *The lord,*
He destroyeth the perfect and the wicked.

Stupid, listen to me: I'm dying

and everywhere there are azaleas and people speaking French,
so many cups of tea I'll never drink!
Job, you are stupid for your faith as we are stupid for our lack of it,
snickering at the stockbroker jogging off the cliff, though
shouldn't we wonder at all a man can endure
to believe, like this one

Whose wife said was so in love
with the world how *could* he look down
while running when he knew
(or should he) all his soul

went up?

Anniversary Song

Look at us there on the museum steps, giggling before the Asian
stone camels and God! The strangers my mother invited to our
    reception.

In photographs spit bubbles out of yellow plastic hoops,
soap suds dive bombing our knee-length chiffons.

If I'd known then what I don't give a hoot about now—
that even the bridesmaids might have preferred to hurl

invectives or Silly Putty at the guests than blush kisses
against our relatives' damp cheeks, that half the drunken

wedding party would later threaten to kill themselves or divorce—
perhaps we wouldn't have allowed ourselves

to be paraded this way. Who were we to be so happy
among our depressed, gay, single friends?

Look: I'm the cloud of cut-rate polyblend champagne
silk flailing in the statue of a marble tire.

You're the slightly more expensive suit hauling me back out.
Woman overboard! What we did for photographs

we also do for love: mug till our webbed eyes cross,
tape condoms to cars under whipped-cream and crepe studs

to fool the gods of fertility. That's the sort of formality
attached to a wedding. *A weeding*

out of the miserable from the less miserable,
as my aunt murmured in the john.

Guess what? Even now, one year later,
we're the less miserable,

grinning at each other like cannibals over the take-out
and new china, slapping each other on the back, chortling

with self-congratulation. Love!
We're still in love! HA HA HA HA!

Look at us giggling in this photograph, side by side astride
the museum's stone camels in our too-tight wedding clothes,

fat whipping under our arms
as we wave, screaming over our fragile luck

in front of God, the gay, and everybody.

25% Pressure

"Of course I support
    women's rights," he
        declared, "along with those

of the criminally
    insane." His lower
        lip trembled, a slug

of red, the vegetarian hands
    looking screwed
        into their wrist sockets.

He didn't mean this
    as a joke. This
        was political earnestness

before women intent
    on teasing him
        at a party—drift of starlings,

our sexual interest
    like a seatide of foam.
        There is nothing worse

to a man than a woman's
    laughter I once read,
        the year my grandmother

bought me the pamphlets
    on rape. A child,
        I read with fascination

the story of a teenager
    whose date suddenly
        pressed her hand

against his jean's crotch,
    then worked her own
        jeans off, forcing her

to lie back
    on the vinyl seat
        that smelled of cigarettes

and breath freshener.
    And I will always remember
        what she wrote next:

Suddenly his penis
    pushed aside my panties
        and he was in me.

Then the quote
    about a woman's laughter,
        its implicit punishment,

its revenge,
    like my revenge
        at this stranger and his lack

of humor. I should say
    he also admitted
        he'd been "pushed aside"

from his job
    when the manager,
        a woman, had reached

for a piece of paper
    and touched his groin
        instead. Pressed it,

actually, he said,
    with full
        "25% pressure."

As if to demonstrate
    what deliberateness
        felt like he struggled

towards my leg
    and turned his palm
        sideways so the branching

knuckles, string
    of fat pears,
        might stroke the skin.

Then thought better
    of it, withdrew
        seeing my eyes fill

with the red light
        of laughter.
                "Don't do that

without—" he began.
        Then he pulled away.
                When I read the account

of the rape
        the first thing I learned
                to believe in was the accident

inherent to sex,
        the pressure
                of thumb or mouth or penis

to act as if knowing
        more than the mind would,
                seeing more than any eye.

I think this man
        felt that too, hating
                the meats and bloods

and shames of him,
        cloistered
                behind a wall of rectitudes.

When he raised his hand
        up to my leg, hovering
                past knee as if to touch

the groin, he stopped
        at the place only ruinors,
                destroyers, numbly

would-be-lovers
        would take. He stopped
                and did not push

past that scrim
    of self-doubt,
        refused to invite despair in

for something simple
    ruined forever.
        What does he know

about his manhood
    but that it might be
        ashamed?

What do I remember
    about the girl in the story?
        The moments before she was raped

she had kissed the boy,
    had leaned up blushing
        to finger his shirt

buttons,
    and laughed, gently,
        in his face.

Death and the Maiden

The Painter

Death cups her to him and his fingers spread
like a web rotting to dust, strung between
the archway of her breasts. Look how her red
lips slightly part under his teeth: her plea
goes unheard by God as the fleshless fingers
twist in her side. Age entered into Eve
this way, through gates of mouth, and hand, and hunger.
Now youth rises like a flight of birds eased
from fields or loosened by a farmer's scythe
in harvest-time. Her arms are smooth and white.
She's beautiful. I've sometimes dreamt of her, her sighs
digging in my mouth, hands reaching from behind
to clasp my back and thighs to her rounded womb.
I wake, choking. *Her body,* I think. *Become a tomb—*

The Maiden

My mother kissed me on the brow: "Aren't you
the lucky one for youth?" Our peat cart moaned
in transit, slowed by her thin fist struck through
with light. Our horse pranced, the wood wheels rolled
among the autumn leaves as peat squares passed
like empty mouths to the hands of customers.
"Consider now the bones and flesh amassed,"
she whispered, "like treasures for the wind." That year
she'd die, and what was I without comfort's uses?
From this thought came the love of love, the body
as a free thing. I make no excuses.
I passed myself like bracelets to an army
of suitors who shared my skin for a pelt.
Go ahead: use me up. I'm an empty mouth myself.

Transplanting

For my mother,
Yoshiko Horikoshi Roripaugh

I. *X-Ray*

My mother carried the chest x-ray
in her lap on the plane, inside
a manila envelope that read
Do Not Bend, and garnished
with leis at the Honolulu Airport
waited in line—this strange image
of ribcage, chain-link vertebrae,
pearled milk of lung and the murky
enigmatic chambers of her heart
in hand. Until it was her turn
and the immigration officer held
the black and white film up
to sun, light pierced clean through
her, and she was ushered from one
life through the gate of another,
wreathed in the dubious and illusory
perfume of plucked orchids.

II. *Ceramic Pig*

Newly arrived in New Mexico,
stiff and crisp in new dungarees,
her honeymoon, they drove
into the mountains in a borrowed car,
spiraling up and up toward the rumor
of deer, into the green tangy turpentine
scent of pine, where air crackled
with the sizzling collision of bees,

furred legs grappling velvet bodies
as they mated mid-air, and where
they came upon the disconsolate gaze
of a Madonna alcoved against
the side of the road, her feet wreathed
in candles, fruit, flowers and other
offerings. Nearby, a vendor
with a wooden plank balanced between
two folding chairs and the glossy
row of ceramic pigs lined up across,
brilliant glaze shimmering the heat.
My mother fell in love with the red
and blue splash of flowers tattooed
into fat flanks and bellies, the green
arabesques of stem and leaf circling
hoof, snout and ear. *So exotic.*
Years later she still describes the pig
with a sigh—*heartbroken,* the word
she chooses with careful consideration.
She'd filled the pig with Kennedy dollars
from the grocery budget, each dollar
a small luxury denied at the local
Piggly Wiggly until one day, jingling
the shift and clink of the pig's
growing silver weight, she shook
too hard, and as if the hoarded wealth
of her future were too much to contain,
the pig broke open—spilling coins
like water, a cold shiny music, into her lap—
fragments of bright pottery shards
scattering delicate as Easter eggshell.

III. *Sneeze*

My mother sneezes in Japanese. *Ke-sho!*
An exclamation of surprise—two sharp
crisp syllables before pulling out
the neatly folded and quartered tissue
she keeps tucked inside the wrist
of her sweater sleeve. Sometimes,

when ragweed blooms, I wonder why
her sneeze isn't mine, why something
so involuntary, so deeply rooted
in the seed of speech, breaks free from
my mouth like thistle in a stiff breeze,
in a language other than my mother's
tongue. How do you chart the diaspora
of a sneeze? *I don't know how*
you turned out this way, she always
tells me, and I think that we are each
her own moon—one face in shadow,
undisclosed seas and surprising mountains,
rotating in the circular music
of separate spheres, but held in orbit
by the gravitational muscle
of the same mercurial spinning heart.

IV. *Dalmatian*

There is an art to this. To shish
kebab the varnished pit of avocado
on three toothpicks above a pickle jar
of cool water, tease down the pale
thirsty hairs of root until one sinewy
arm punches up and unclenches its green
fisted hand, palm open, to the sun.
To discern the oniony star-struck
subterfuge of bulbs, their perverse
desires, death-like sleeps, and conspire
behind the scenes to embroider
the Elizabethan ruffles and festoons
of their flamboyant resurrections.
To trick the tomatoes into letting down
their swelling, tumescent orbs
in the cottony baked heat of the attic
until their sunburnt faces glow
like round orange lanterns under
the crepuscular twilight of the eaves.
Unwrapping the cuttings of succulents
from their moist, paper towel bandages,

and snugging them down into firm
dimples of dirt and peat, coaxing up
the apple-green serpentine coils of sweet
pea with a snake charmer's song to wind
around the trellis and flicker their quick
pink petaled tongues. The tender slips
of mint, sueded upturned bells of petunia,
and slim fingers of pine that pluck
the metal window screen like a tin harp
by the breakfast nook where my father
stirs his morning coffee and waits
for the neighbors' Dalmatian to hurl
itself over the back fence and hang,
limply twisting and gasping on the end
of its chain and collar like a polka-dotted
petticoat, until my father goes outside
and takes its baleful kicking weight
in his arms and gently tosses it back
over the fence into the neighbors' yard.
Year after year, the dandelions
and clover are weeded out, summers
come and go, and roots stubbornly inch
down around the foundation of the house—
labyrinthine, powerful and deep.

V. *Japanese Apple*

She was given an apple on the plane,
round and fragrant with the scent
of her grandfather's fruit orchards
during autumn, when chestnuts
dropped from their trees and struck
the metal rooftop like the small heavy
tongues of bells, and black dragon-
flies like quick shiny needles darted
in and out of the spin and turn
of leaves fluttering down like soft
bright scraps of silk. She wrapped
the apple in a napkin to save
for later, and it was confiscated

at customs before she had the chance
for even a taste. Over the years it
seemed to grow larger, yellower, juicier
and more delicious, and even though
there were burnished rows of apples
stacked in gleaming pyramids
at the supermarket with quaint
names like Macintosh, Winesap,
and Granny Smith, and even though
there were sunlit apple orchards
at my American grandfather's ranch,
where rattlesnakes slumbered
in the heat and redolence of fruit
flesh, frightening the horses,
she sampled one after another
but they never tasted as sweet
or as bright as the apple taken from her,
the one she had to leave behind.

Hope

There are nights I dream of goldfish
and in my dreams they sing to me in
fluted, piercing sopranos like the Vienna
Boys Choir. Although in the daylight
they are mostly silent and ravenous—
the suction-cup grip of their mouths
on my fingertip like tiny rubber bath-
room plungers when they rise to strike
at an offering of chopped green peas.
Sometimes a frenetic clicking of marbles
nosed and nudged across the aquarium
floor during scavenging sessions for food,
sounding like the rack and crack of a game
of pool. Such hunger. Such extravagance.

Their ovoid bodies are like Faberge eggs
filigreed with flakes of hammered gold,
a glittering armor of polished gill
plates, their dorsal fins elegant ribbed
silk fans that open when in motion,
and fold themselves shut in repose.
Clever pectoral fins maneuver and oscillate
like small propellers, and the circling
tails flare and twirl with the hypnotic
flourish of the toreador's cape. All
is endless metaphor here. All of it.

I once read the goldfish memory span
was three seconds, and does this mean
each moment is an astonishment
in a series of quick incarnations spiraling
outward the way water ripples away
from a disturbance, so that, in the end,
each brief flicker of awareness
is long enough to learn to simply *be*,
and isn't this really, after all, enough?

One morning I woke to find the red-capped
oranda in distress—fins clamped sadly
down, listless tail, gasping on the back
corner floor of the aquarium. I netted
her and put her in a glass bowl sugared
with a quarter cup of sea salt crystals—
the way my Japanese grandfather once
showed my mother, and the way my mother,
years later in America, once showed me.

And several hours later, the sheer veils
of tail and fin began to bloom, to resume
their arabesques and veronicas around
the sleek shimmer of her white satin body—
the scandal of her scarlet cap dipping
coquettishly, onyx beads of eyes swiveling
in their turquoise socket rings. She swam
around and around the clear glass bowl,
until my heart swung left and followed her
around and around from above the way
red-throated loons on the Island of Seto
circle and follow the fishing boats, tamed
by the fishermen, and calling out
with their strange and mournful cries.

Dream Carp

People traveled from miles away to see
my paintings of fish—
the jeweled armor of their scales, the beadlike

set of their eyes in
rubbery socket rings, the glimmering
swish of fin and tail

so real it seemed that you could almost dip
a net deep into
the paper and pull up the arching wet

weight of a golden carp,
a shiny trout, or the dark muscular
heft of a bass with

its mouth stretched into the surprised, wiry
"oh" of a child's wind-
sock. I captured my models from the sea,

lake, and goldfish pond
in the back garden, so careful not to
let their mouths be torn

by the hook, their scales chipped, or the silky
tissue of their tails
ripped by a clumsy hand. I kept them in

large glass bowls, fed them
mosquito wings or dry silkworm pupas
offered from chopsticks,

and when I was finished making sketches,
I quickly took them
back and set them free again. Every

night I dream I swim
with these fish as a golden carp—black spots
on cloisonné scale

pulled to the surface by the deceptive
creamy luster of
the moon or the sizzle of firefly lights

across the water.
And every night I am tempted once
again by the smell

of the baited hook, by my predictable
hunger for earthly
things, and each time I am surprised again

by the stinging hook
in my lip that pulls me mercilessly
into the bright air,

setting my gills on fire, the sharp, silver
pain of the knife that
slits me open so easily from tail

to throat to reveal
the scarlet elastic of my raw gills,
the translucent film

of my air sac, the milky rise of my
stomach, and the gray
marbled coil of my intestines. I rise

late each day, and work
in brighter light. When I die, I will
have my painting brought

down to the lake and slipped into the water.
First the edges of
ink will blur, and then there will be a great

flurry as the fins,
tails and bodies begin blossoming in-
to life again, each

fish detaching from its canvas of silk
or rice paper—a
swirl of color, motion, swimming away.

Brenda Shaughnessy

Rise

I can't believe you've come back,
like the train I missed so badly, barely,
which stopped & returned for me. It scared me,
humming backwards along the track.

I rise to make a supper succulent
for the cut of your mouth, your bite of wine
so sharp, you remember you were mine.
You may resist, you will relent.

At home in fire, desire is bread
whose flour, water, salt, and yeast,
not yet confused, are still, at least,
in the soil, the sea, the mine, the dead.

I have all I longed for, you
in pleasure. You missed me, your body swelling.
Once more, you lie with me, smelling
of almonds, as the poisoned do.

Your One Good Dress

should never be light. That kind of thing feels
like a hundred shiny-headed waifs backlit
and skeletal, approaching. Dripping and in
unison, murmuring, "We *are* you."

No. And the red dress (think about it,
redress) is all neckhole. The brown
is a big wet beard with, of course, a backslit.
You're only as sick as your secrets.

There is an argument for the dull-chic,
the dirty olive and the Cinderelly. But those
who exhort it are only part of the conspiracy:
"Shimmer, shmimmer," they'll say. "Lush, shmush."

Do not listen. It's a part of the anti-obvious
movement and it's sheer matricide. Ask your mum.
It would kill her if you were ewe gee el why.
And it is a crime to wonder, am I. In the dark a dare,

Am I now. You put on your Niña, your Pinta, your
Santa María. Make it simple to last your whole
life long. Make it black. Glassy or deep.
Your body is opium and you are its only true smoker.

This black dress is your one good dress.
Bury your children in it. Visit your pokey
hometown friends in it. Go missing for days.
Taking it off never matters. That just wears you down.

Postfeminism

There are two kinds of people, soldiers and women,
as Virginia Woolf said. Both for decoration only.

Now that is too kind. It's technical: virgins and wolves.
We have choices now. Two little girls walk into a bar,

one orders a Shirley Temple. Shirley Temple's pimp
comes over and says you won't be sorry. She's a fine

piece of work but she don't come cheap. Myself, I'm
in less fear of predators than of walking around

in my mother's body. That's sneaky, that's more
than naked. Let's even it up: you go on fuming in your

gray room. I am voracious alone. Blank and loose,
metallic lingerie. And rare black-tipped cigarettes

in a handmade basket case. Which of us weaves
the world together with a quicker blur of armed

seduction: your war-on-thugs, my body stockings.
Ascetic or carnivore. Men will crack your glaze

even if you leave them before morning. Pigs
ride the sirens in packs. Ah, flesh, technoflesh,

there are two kinds of people. Hot with mixed
light, drunk with insult. You and me.

Panopticon

My bedroom window can be seen from the viewing deck
of the World Trade Center. I've seen it.
What I saw?

My roommate experimenting with my vibrator.
She looked lovely through sheer curtains
on my creamy bed. Is she thinking of me?

I am thinking of her and I left bread crumbs on the telepath.
She can feel it, my seeing, even through a trance of fog.
I've lit her with it.

It is her blindfold, her sweet curse, her ration
of privacy spilled like flour as she imagines
the miraculous bread is rising.

I decided on three possible reactions:

To keep watching her and, when I go home, to mention
the strange vision I had, describing
what I saw in detail.

                    To feed the telescope with quarter
after quarter, and read a book while the time ticks.
I have been blessed with seeing, as with a third eye,
without the compulsive mimesis of appearing. The luxury
of an octopus is never using any legs for walking.

                    Or, to stay home with my own
pair of binoculars, in the dark, watching whoever is
watching me, watch me.

Interior with Sudden Joy

    [after a painting by Dorthea Tanning]

To come into my room is to strike strange.
My plum velvet pillow & my hussy spot
the only furniture.

Red stripes around my ankles, tight
as sisters. We are maybe fourteen, priceless
with gooseflesh.

Our melon bellies, our mouths of tar. Us four:
my mud legged sister, my bunched-up self,
the dog & the whirligig just a prick on the eye.

We are all sewn in together, but the door is open.
The book is open too. You must write in red
like Jesus and his friends.

Be my other sister, we'll share a mouth.
We'll split the dress
down the middle, our home, our Caesarian.

When the Bishop comes he comes
diagonal, from the outside, & is a lie.
He comes to bless us all with cramps,

mole on the chin that he is,
to bring us the red something,
a glow, a pumping.

Not softly a rub with loincloth
& linseed. More of a beating,
with heart up the sleeve.

He says, *The air in here is tight & sore*
but punctured, sudden, by a string quartet.
We are! In these light-years we've wrung a star.

I am small for my age.
Child of vixenwood, lover of the color olive
and its stain.

I live to leave, but I never either.
One leg is so long we can all walk it.
Outside is a thousand bitten skins

and civilization its own murder of crows.
I am ever stunned,
seduced whistle-thin

& hot with home. Breathless with
mercury, columbine. Come, let us miss
another wintertime.

The English Canon

It's not that the first speakers left out women
Unless they were goddesses, harlots, or impossible loves
Seen from afar, often while bathing,

And it's not that the only parts my grandfathers could have played
Were as extras in Xanadu,
Nor that it gives no instructions for shopping or cooking.

The trouble is, I've spent my life
Getting over the lyrics
That taught me to brush my hair till it's gleaming,

Stay slim, dress tastefully, and not speak of sex,
Death, violence, or the desire for any of them,
And to let men do the talking and warring

And bringing of the news. I know a girl's got to protest
These days, but she also has to make money
And do her share of journalism and combat,

And she has to know from the gut whom to trust,
Because what do her teachers know, living in books,
And what does she know, starting from scratch?

Female Infanticide: A Guide for Mothers

in order of expediency

I

Ultrasound, abortion.

II

Drowning; asphyxiation.

III

Hilltop abandonment.

IV

Automobile accident.

V

Failure to immunize; ill nutrition.

VI

Lack of activity; inattention.

VII

Care by little-known relations.

VIII

A mixup on a family vacation.

IX

Wait until you have a son;
put the female up for adoption.

X

Create a scandal in her adolescence.
Her options: suicide, disappearance.

XI

Raise her as one of her brother's servants;
marry her off at your convenience.

XII

Keep her unwed (use psychological torture).
In old age a daughter is fine good fortune.

Savannah Crabs

Bluish and thirsty, packed tight as oranges,
they come from the coast in the iced trunk
of the blue Buick our aunt drives. She's sunk
in thoughts of dinner and not the tinges

of dread that will stain her African violets
as she tends a back pain. She does not think
of her mother, who'll die this fall under pink
bedclothes without a goodnight; the eyelets

of her gown will spell the Chinese words
for *loneliness, lovelessness, white birds.*

When our aunt and her passengers get to town,
my brother and I crouch by the crate,
poke slow ones with sticks. Two escape;
our parents chase them with tongs around

the garden, then dump all seventy-four
in the laundry-room sink. They scuttle and flip
like fat gymnasts; they amaze us kids.
We salt them, singing *When it rains it pours.*

They spit back curses: *You'll ache; you'll smother;
you'll never be able to talk to each other.*

My aunt has brought me a spiny, off-yellow
shell, big as my hand. It sits
on the dryer, where I forget about it
to watch the steamer, where waving hello

and goodbye, the first mute batch reddens
and stills. I think of my shell and go back.
Out of it, welt-ridden legs grasp
no sand. He's ugly, a hermit, threatening.

I peer in his house and read the prophecy:
You'll find joy, but you must leave the family.

Wedding Gifts

Everywhere, a reason for caution:
crystal bowls, white teacups, porcelain.

Objects, which used to tumble in
on their way to the junk heap,
now possessed origins.

I had no idea what to do with a dog
that didn't come from the pound,

and now, as if suddenly old,
found frailties in places I never knew existed.
Casseroles leapt, glasses imploded—

I wept each time. I knew from poetry
that no one conquers entropy,

but I also knew from poetry
everyone has to try. Rescued, the animal
loses all anonymity

in a syllable, and the hero's nobility
dissolves into family.

Marriage is the same, with dishes and rings.
Vows or no vows, you embrace your own death,
journeying to which, you only get clumsier, and things,

which you thought mere material,
become irreplaceable.

Bird of Paradise Aubade with Bangkok
Etching over the Bed

Woke to hear you refuse
to stop working in heavy rain, shoveling the mud
that beggars our part
of the yard. After a while, I heard the rasp of iron's
rake on gravel, wet earth, your bending for the gaps
to get the seedlings right. Then for hours from the window

I watched all your muscles connecting up, your body's parse
of sweat and salt, hollows
between the ribs appearing, then not, around your
breath's steady reed and thrum. Watched,
you see, until I knew, for once, I wouldn't try to leave.
Though I did want to walk out and say something else

about moving through the myth
of ask and answer once. I wanted to tell you how I saw it spill
out on sidewalk, alleyway, underpass, and how traveling
that way, in another country,
I had to love the hawkers' come ons,
their peddling, every night, the Leda and swan–style

tracings. On our wall now, I can make out her limbs
misted in chalk blear, the thighs streaked, but still skirting his will.
And when you come in I want to show you
the half man, half bird, the one whose mouth
hangs open, his little razor-cut hungering of how much
he wants her. Or have you see how a span

of white rivers between
them, the distance of missing they wed again
and again. The chalk drifts through
the design. Outside, a real bird's rapid trill in flight
skirts the window frame. And now you're stepping over
the lawn's dropped

branches, carrying the tallest stalks still hung with weeds.
Getting there, you say, giving me the ones almost in bloom.
After you turn away
I put the buds to my mouth
to taste the skin before it breaks open, the bodies, newly green,
bound to root-pact, stem-line, moments before they fall.

Comings and Goings
(Bangkok)

Once, in a house I will inherit in a land I can't explain,
    I heard the shout

of meat bones offered up from the market where it all goes
                wholesale. Actually, the morning's

heat rose from the newly paved road—thin folds debuting
        into the visible—

and much later, children were called in, one by one,
        away from, because of,

the street. All day, from somewhere beyond the billboard
            of a woman amply

luring tourists to new tastes, came the sound of temple monks
            praying for their one wish—

born wanting to be born again. I'd been told their voices'
        tidal heave and dwindle

would pay the debt, in part, to whatever local god they used
                to conjure creation,

giving it their good deeds, right notes, in- and exhalings,
            short spans of the body.

Meanwhile, this week in this world, a mound of sludge and leaf rot
        caught behind the house is,

over a week's time, veiled and parceled out among
                the red ants. And still

the black flies keep entering and exiting the air above
            the table's day-old

bowl of plums. I'd like to know how it's good, or enough, for anyone—
        this small rush into

the sickly sweet, these brief becomings, part of the increase
                we call ourselves by,

since there's also the ten-year-old girl I recognize and hardly know,
            the one who's hired to sweep and clean,

to rid us of the dirt tracked in, and bundled out, finding the floor's
        small shames. Dust clumps,

carpet threads, the bits of fallen meat scraps, all the S-shaped hair
                that daily, secretly

escaped. What can she inherit in this country where they speak
            three languages,

one for their betters, another for family, a last for servants:
    millions of voices

pitched toward the accidents of birth? I know she could leave us
              like some of the others

who wandered down the road for a better sum in the massage parlor
         they also call a coffee shop.

Or could be dreaming already, as she sweeps, of the barker who calls
      each of the girls

by number, so that, by turns, every one is among the chosen.
              He's there, behind the strobe,

passing the bodies between one dark and the next, generation
        after generation.

And she is here for now, mid-afternoon, her small hips swing
      a slow bargain with the heat.

As if this dust shaken from her broom could enter
              the fragile argument,

we watch the freed traces scatter in sun, then cling briefly to grass.
        I look up, then look away.

To My Cousin in Bangkok, Age 16

What space is for, to the boy peddling
through smoke and traffic blast,
past curry stalls and lean-to yard
encampments, is to keep in place
the dreams of the dead. Each night
his mother, long gone, appears to him
with the same command, saying get up,
go out, take the ride now, so that mornings
he snakes across the city to the old house
that was once theirs. Out to tend what little
remains from her life among the living,
he comes crashing through last year's
pile of peach and lychee cans, wrappers
bleared by heat below the carport, and goes
inside to dust the table's one blue bowl.
He shoves his fingers down into the fuchsia
broken open beside the windowsill, moves
the TV from porch to den and back again,
trying to remember what she wanted.
It takes all day to work these increments
of an intimate geography he'd like,
just once, to get right. Because there is always

behind him, you see, the one time he didn't.
Night his mother lay dying, he beside the bed,
there's the moment when she stopped
shaking and he made his first mistake,
thinking now she'll be all right. As she went
cold he covered her body with more blankets,
so she could sleep, and after that he left.
How the room must have darkened then,
small bed filling with that new weight.
And now if he comes back, fills the bowl
on her table with clear water, gauging
its cold for a second in this house
where he was born, the one she gave him,
it's to test his bit of the absolute, plunging
his hands, almost a man's, into the blue.

Stillborn

Mother, here's what the night offers: silence,
    a tree with no bird, four unlit lamps, one sink's
empty bowl, and my closets packed with the spilt,
    open mouths of shoes. I'm up again at 3 A.M.,
one year past the age you made me. Inside
    my small apartment, a sleeve of winged
ants spun from the day's heat has expired
    by now. I brush their bodies, cramped as raisins,
from the windowsill. . . . A moment ago, hearing
    a rumbling truck's distant effort
to take the upgrade, and then nothing,
    I saw the black of an oak tree outside
set against the lesser dark of a city-lit
    sky, and hated its outline of absence.
Or not hated, feared becoming. Look, even if I want
    to write the names of everyone
I love on the dark, I still can't say

I know or understand the poverty
	of your grief that summer just like this one
when the doctor, knowing the baby inside
	you—the one before me—was dead, sent you home
without saying anything was wrong. Later,
	you said, he spoke to the husband—my father,
although that wasn't to be for years—
	because he thought the right man should break the news
gently. And tonight I keep picturing
	your interim hours, vacuuming
the carpet, turning the TV on, then off,
	then on again, reaching that much wider
past the couch, making way for your laden midriff.
	Meanwhile, the truth in the room with you,
not yet spoken, a nothing you couldn't know
	your body still wrapped itself around. . . .

Until he came home. Until the long car ride
	to the hospital for shots that could lift
your mind from consciousness and the final
	suction. Afterward, I can see you
walking through the sorrow of those days,
	threading the Washington parks. The late
August there spawns so many traces
	of gray that color's ghosted, a wish
you've given up on. I've thought of you each
	stepping through that mud, avoiding
the dropped pods of magnolia, the paths'
	thinning sprays of crepe myrtle,
not speaking of the phantom child
	you would also have named "Pimone,"
my sibling, my slanted self,
	already the unborn fact of his male sex
wasted by then, part seahorse,
	part flattened snail, a damp-rotted tuber.
I wish we could tell one another
	what it is the stubborn flesh asks of us.
For now, all the issue I can offer
	is to dedicate the silence of this night

to you and the shadow child who wasn't
　　let to swim for the shore of his own voice,
the one who taught how little you could get
　　from the botched scrawl of matter. . . . Mother,
on a blank page, in elegy, every day,
　　I could write my name and erase it.
It's six o'clock. A few new ants furrow
　　the sill's cracks and outside, sunrise,
another one, leeches in through the oak limbs.
　　If I look up, the windowpane,
transparent, gives me back my face.
　　Enough, Mother. Almost enough.

Winter Swim

Less to improve her body than to trick
its talent for pain, my mother drives her daily
miles beneath tree limbs swagged with snow,
strips herself of street clothes in the pine
and faintly pee-scented locker room, and pulls
the slick coral suit over her loosening flesh
for the work of yet another immersion.
This is what she trusts: her lungs
and how far they will take her, training
to follow the pool's scrawled underbelly
of blue lines until she can swim a full
forty seconds before turning to inhale.
And because she tries to make the smallest faiths
burgeon to a kind of science, she posits.
however unlikely, that even in this dreary
immaculate, made so by chlorine, a bit
can rinse away—if only the cramp of constant
gravity, the ache of her two surgeries.

"You see," the doctor said, "some motion,
some activity. . . ." Though no one ever says
you need some relief from the common drudgeries,
from a lifetime's mild and major humiliations:
housework, failed marriages, the cyclical
stains of the body, the new dog's vomit
in your shoes. I too, want to believe
in her bargain with the pool's surface,
the private sacs beneath her ribs
filling, emptying, filling with air.
It's only what we might wish for anyone
loved, that even their simple routines
can become ritual, bathed in some sweetness
of meaning. Her arms lift easily up
and over. She kicks under to retrieve
the forgotten prop of a child's game, a quarter's
glint from the ten-foot marker, lane three. . . .

Last week, during the dishes, I listened in
when her family called from the other side
of the world to say now they were waiting
for her father to die. She could hear
the sister repeating across pacific
lines, he might go at any time and I'm
sorry. Slowly, we understood how his own
body's blood and lungs had surged, that night
and day, beyond the likelihood of more life.
There was nothing left but to wait
in the brief swell of his remaining.

And that's where we left it, for the time being,
the dial tone seeming to fall away from her ears
as she looked past the kitchen window's
frozen scrim. For a long time she didn't move.
I could see her face, the ice filings pinned
to the glass, and beyond that, the yard's frozen pond.

I wish I could have said something.
I wish I could have held her body to me,
fiercely then, as if we weren't made
of simple fluid and the limits of that grace,
as if she could never dim and be stilled.
Or else pushed her out to the pond's frozen
currency to watch the cold-dulled carp
we had wintering beneath an ice sheet.
In this season, they're like a fine middle
that doesn't seem to ask for more—but gets it—
each a coral or bone-blue slipper,
suspended, able to be slicked back,
with a single thaw, into the small riot of swimming.

But I said nothing and made no move
since they were beautiful,
and because of that they were useless.
Even if I had walked out to the solid edge
and called her name,
she could not have come.

25th & Dolores

One could search this landscape in vain
for signs of necessity. From here
just the gently tumbled houses,

the tall white hospital, a garland
of palm trees reeling down the avenue,
and a bright scuffed sky the body

keeps mistaking for grieving.
The calla lilies are one form of life.
How they persist in their slow

unwelling, how they define
luxury as the absence of threat.
"The most beautiful freeway

in America" is beginning
to the right: its heaped-up hills,
its full-strength sunlight burning off

the camphor-infused fog.
You were wrong. I'm still capable
of begging. Crook your arm

around my neck, knees behind
my knees, and march me downhill
into the standing water.

Décor

My covetous eye casts over you,
taking you apart. I'd like a trophy of you
for every room of the house.

The bend of your cocked wrist
in the join of a rafter to the wall;
an eyebrow floated in a cut-glass bowl;

and instead of an antimacassar
draping my overstuffed chair,
a crochet netting of your veins.

Something authoritative,
asymmetrical, perhaps
a bit outré. Featuring that spiral-

shaped mystery of gravitation,
making the room attend it,
composed, aware of distances.

What better in my front hall
with its fan light, its tall
mirrors, than the immaculate

roundness of your plump heel
and toes—substantial, rococo,
a handle for my front door:

warm to the touch,
it turns easily, opens. . . .
You can go now.

Korean Martyrs

Where was it we went that night?
That long, low building: floodlights
rimmed in lavender, the moon ringed
in rose. I would rather, then, have stayed

outside, where spider webs glowed
like jellyfish in the damp yew hedges,
where the paths were chalky pebbles
set with giant stepping stones.

But the film was starting. In the air-
conditioned dark, a crowd of strangers,
strange families (not from our church)
in rows of metal folding chairs to see

a man quartered by horses: strain
stitched across his shining back
then, all over at once, an unraveling
and then the spill of meat;

a girl pushed through a doorway
naked among the soldiers:
she grew a dress to cover herself,
a blue dress with a blinding sash.

Venice, Unaccompanied

    Waking
on the train I thought
we were attacked

    by light:
chrome-winged birds
hatching from the lagoon.

That first day
the buoys were all
that made the harbor

   bearable:
pennies sewn into a hemline.
Later I learned to live in it,

   to walk
through the alien city—
a bee-keeper's habit—

   with fierce light
clinging to my head and hands.
Treated as gently as every

   other guest—
each house's barbed antennae
trawling for any kind

   of weather—
still I sobbed in a glass box
on an unswept street

   with the last
few lire ticking like fleas
off my phonecard *I'm sorry*

   I can't
stand this, which
one of us do you love?

Flatlanders

Here the sky's all spreading belly,
postcoital, pressing the ground
deeper into the ground.

Rumors of incest: a folded
Rorschach, a mirror in love with a lake.

In fenced backyards across Fort Bend County
buttered-up high school sweethearts
lie on sheets of tinfoil for a tan;

wake up crying, siren-red,
eyelids swollen into temporary lips.

     *

We know no other shapes
than those that contain us;
we have built our zoneless city,

hub of freeways, a dark étoile.
In Tony's, an ageless lady stirs

her iced tea till the ice cubes melt
to sharp-boned shadows of themselves;
a wink of lime slice, her gem-knuckled hand.

In the garage of St. Joseph's Children's Hospital,
shivering, an intern in short-sleeved scrubs

pulls a soft gold spot into the center
of his cigarette filter, an indrawn breath.

     *

Hurricane season in the suburbs:
windows asterisked

with masking tape—cross hairs,
false-eyelashed eyes. We remember

when the whole city was a pavé brooch
most of us would covet.
Sometimes we feel lucky:
the hurricane's eye—

our shy neighbors emerge
into the ultramarine
spotlight, the settling leaves,

stand hushed, reverent,
peering up the skirts of the storm.

    *

In the eighth grade we learned
a cone pushed through a plane
is a spreading circle to the Flatlanders.

There's no point in looking up.
From time to time a football drops

from the technicolor buzz of stadium lights
into the supplicant hands
of some misshapen archetypal hero.

And on the last night of every year,
the sullen boot-clad men of Pasadena

park on the feeder roads, sit for hours
on the roofs of their pickups

trying to shoot the fireworks out of the sky.

C. Dale Young

The Philosopher in Florida

Midsummer lies on this town
like a plague: locusts now replaced
by humidity, the bloodied Nile

now an algae-covered rivulet
struggling to find its terminus.
Our choice is a simple one:

to leave or to remain, to render
the Spanish moss a memory
or to pull it from trees, repeatedly.

And this must be what the young
philosopher felt, the pull of a dialectic so basic
the mind refuses, normally,

to take much notice of it.
Outside, beyond a palm-tree fence,
a flock of ibis mounts the air,

our concerns ignored
by their quick white wings.
Feathered flashes reflected in water,

the bending necks of the cattails:
the landscape feels nothing—
it repeats itself with or without us.

Broughtonia

IN MEMORY OF F.C. (1965–91),
WHO DIED OF AIDS COMPLICATIONS

But there under the dark eaves
of rain forest, we found *Broughtonia,*
its crimson petals aflame,
its yellow throat, veins hinting purple,

rising to a sanguine corolla surrounded
by sepals as crinkled as mourning crepe.
We followed a path lengthened slash by slash,
the islanders swinging machetes in front of us.

We were told how Broughton's hands trembled
when he sighted those orchids languishing;
as he sketched, his nervous pencil
exaggerated the crumpled edge of every bloom.

We too had learned to exaggerate.
That night in Montego Bay,
we told the others we had seen dozens;
in New York, we said hundreds.

Today, we might have imagined the wind
licking us back into the Gully,
our hands as uninhibited as those petals.
No. I can no longer imagine. I choose not to.

Exile

Clothed only by the sound of the sea,
we stood naked on our balcony, masters
of all that lay before us, the green life

of the croquet lawn dotted again
and again by the cultured hibiscus,
its blooms the ready medium

of the master pointillist (read: *gardener*)
who now takes lessons from no one
but the river that has nurtured gardens

far more exotic than this, and on the sides
of cliffs, no less, as if to flaunt its virtuosity.
At that hour, even the handful of glare

left over from midday had to succumb
to the sound of the sea, its tireless percussion.
Sanded, our dark skin darker,

we had climbed seventy-four steps
into the heart of the palazzo, our suite
the necessary haven, the fort

we create no matter where we live.
And so, exhausted by the sun, we stood there,
two men among shadows, the sunlight

kept at bay by leaves, the two of us staring
at coconuts bobbing in the surf, strange skulls
trying their damnedest to remind us of nothing.

Moonlight Cocktail

A couple of jiggers of moonlight
And add a star
Pour in the blue of a June night
And one guitar...

Late afternoon, the sky is almost as blue
as a sapphire martini, blue pulled into ether—
how many martinis will make me blue to you?
Ray Eberle's vocals take us back to 1941,

uniforms and the War but nothing tangible,
nothing until he sings of the moon.
On a moonless June night years ago,
we drove out to Cedar Key despite midnight

approaching, sat in a playground and talked
about the moon. Even then, sitting on a swing,
I had fallen for the sound of your voice
hushed by the breakers and the wind in the trees.

But beginnings are always this way:
a jigger or two of the expected and a splash
of something blue, the good friend
you take with you on a nighttime drive

and the feel of his lips as he kisses your neck.
Lying at the foot of the bed last night reading,
you were half-naked but clothed in bright light.
Despite all the years, I still study you.

Outside the bar, just over your shoulder,
the city sits under a darkening sky
and a new moon is making an appearance—
even now, we talk about the moon.

Invective

From the Turnpike, north-central Florida,
the body in transit can sight a red dirt road
climbing a small hill, and yes, it cannot help
but note the final turn before that road

vanishes in skyline and emptiness.
There in the car, another lesson in vantage.

What next? A lesson about the weather?
The impending front? Abstraction was coming,
and the signs along the road said to make ready,
start now, repent. But not even abstraction

could have stopped what was already happening:
red the dirt road in Florida, red the bauxite-laden

dirt of Mandeville, Jamaica, fifty years earlier,
my father walking up a hill utterly unimpressed
with the red earth there beneath his feet.
Had I, too, been conditioned? Hardened?

Every patient in my study died in two years,
and what had I done, presented the facts

at a conference, answered questions
about protocols and confidence intervals?
I used to tell the dead about dying.
Now I search for crude metaphors, like this dirt.

Acknowledgments

The editor is grateful for permission to reprint the following poets' work:

Lisa Asagi: "April 14," "April 15," and "April 22" first appeared in *Twelve Scenes from 12 A.M.* (Tinfish Press) by Lisa Asagi and Gaye Chan. © 2001 by Lisa Asagi. Reprinted by permission of Tinfish Press. "Soundtrack for Home Movie No. 3" reprinted by permission of the author.

Rick Barot: "Reading Plato," "Bird Notes," "Bonnard's Garden," "Occupations," and "At Point Reyes" are reprinted from *The Darker Fall* (Sarabande Books) by Rick Barot. © 2002 by Rick Barot. Reprinted by permission of Sarabande Press and the author. "Reading Plato" first appeared in *Black Warrior Review.* "Bird Notes" first appeared in *Grand Street.* "Bonnard's Garden" first appeared in *Ploughshares.* "Occupations" first appeared in *Poetry.* "At Point Reyes" first appeared in the *New England Review.*

Nick Carbó: "American Adobo," "The Bronze Dove," "Ang Tunay Lalaki Stalks the Streets of New York," "Ang Tunay Na Lalaki Is Baffled by Cryptic Messages," and "Ang Tunay Na Lalaki Visits His Favorite Painting" from *Secret Asian Man* (Tia Cucha Press) by Nick Carbó. © 1995 by Tia Chucha Press and Nick Carbó. Reprinted by permission of the author. "Ang Tunay Lalaki Stalks the Streets of New York" first appeared in *Flippin': Filipinos on America.* Reprinted by permission of the author. "Ang Tunay Na Lalaki Is Baffled by Cryptic Messages" first appeared in *Asian Pacific American Journal.*

Jennifer Chang: "The Sign Reads:" "Swindled, I Left Everything," "If There Is No Memory, It Did Not Happen," "What the Landscape Works For Is What I Have Left," and "I *Am* in Unction *Now*" reprinted by permission of the author. "I Remember Her, a Bowl of Water" appeared in *Beloit Poetry Journal* (Winter 2002/2003). Reprinted by permission of the author.

Tina Chang: "Origin & Ash" appeared in *Ploughshares* (Spring 2000). Reprinted by permission of the author. "Invention" appeared in *Callaloo* (Summer 1997). Reprinted by permission of the author. "Fish Story" appeared in *Asian Pacific American Journal* (Fall 1996). Reprinted by permission of the author. "Versions" reprinted by permission of the author. "Curriculum" appeared in the *Missouri Review* (Spring 1998). Reprinted by permission of the author. "Journal of the Diabetic Father" appeared in *Asian American Renaissance Journal* (Fall 1996). Reprinted by permission of the author.

Marilyn Chin: "How I Got That Name" from *Phoenix Gone, the Terrace Empty* (Milkweed Press) by Marilyn Chin. © 1994 by Marilyn Chin. Reprinted by permission of Milkweed Press.

Oliver de la Paz: "Manong Jose . . . ," "When Fidelito Is the New Boy at School," "Grounding," "Carpenter Ants," and "Nine Secrets the Recto Family Can't Tell the Boy" from *Names above Houses* (Southern Illinois University Press) by Oliver de la Paz. © 2001 by Oliver de la Paz. Reprinted by permission of Southern Illinois University Press. "Nine Secrets . . ." first appeared in *Quarterly West.*

Marisa de los Santos: "October: One Year Later," "First Light," "Because I Love You," and "Woman Reading" from *From the Bones Out* (University of South Carolina Press) by Marisa de los Santos. © 2000 by Marisa de los Santos. Reprinted by permission of the author and the University of South Carolina Press. "First Light" first appeared in *Chelsea.* Reprinted by permission of the author. "Because I Love You" first appeared in *Poetry.* Reprinted by permission of the author. "Rite of Passage" reprinted by permission of the author.

Brian Komei Dempster: "Measure" appeared in *Quarterly West* (Spring/Summer 2001). Reprinted by permission of the author. "Exposure" appeared in *Gulf Coast* (Winter/Spring 2002). Reprinted by permission of the author. "The Pink House in Four Variations" and "The Burning" reprinted by permission of the author.

Linh Dinh: "The Fox Hole," "The Most Beautiful Word," "Earth Cafeteria," and "Longitudes" from *All Around What Empties Out* (Tinfish Press) by Linh Dinh. © 2002 by Linh Dinh. Reprinted by permission of the author and Tinfish Press. "The Fox Hole" first appeared in *Brooklyn Rail* and *Drunkard Boxing* (Singing Horse Press, 1998) by Linh Dinh. "The Most Beautiful Word" first appeared in *X-Connect* and in *Drunkard Boxing.* "The Most Beautiful Word" was also anthologized in *Best American Poetry 2000,* © 2000 by Linh Dinh and Scribner, and *Great American Prose Poems: From Poe to the Present,* © 2003 by Linh Dinh and Scribner. "Earth Cafeteria" first appeared in the *Chicago Review* and *Of Vietnam: Identities in Dialogue* (Palgrave, 2002). "Longitudes" first appeared in *A Small Triumph over Lassitude* (Leroy Press, 2001) by Linh Dinh.

Monica Ferrell: "Persephone" appeared in the *Paris Review.* Reprinted by permission of the author. "In the Grips of a Sickness Transmitted by Wolves" and "The Fire of Despair" appeared in the *New England Review.* Reprinted by permission of the author. "In the Binary Alleys of the Lion's Virus" reprinted by permission of the author.

Cathy Park Hong: "All the Aphrodisiacs," "Assiduous Rant," "During Bath," and "Not Henry Miller but Mother" from *Translating Mo'um* (Hanging Loose Press) by Cathy Park Hong. © 2002 by Cathy Park Hong. Reprinted by permission of the author and Hanging Loose Press. "All the Aphrodisiacs" first appeared in *Mudfish Journal.* Reprinted by permission of the author.

Antonio Jocson: "Lot's Wife," "The Hen," "Bamiyan," "Early Morning under Persimmon," and "Crèvecoeur" reprinted by permission of the author.

Vandana Khanna: "Train to Agra," "Spell," "The India of Postcards," "Two Women," and "Alignment" from *Train to Agra* (Southern Illinois University Press) by Vandana Khanna. © 2001 by Vandana Khanna. Reprinted by permission of the author and Southern Illinois University Press. "Spell" first appeared in *Callaloo*. Reprinted by permission of the author. "The India of Postcards" first appeared in *Crab Orchard Review*. Reprinted by permission of the author. "Alignment" first appeared in *Hanging Loose*. Reprinted by permission of the author.

Suji Kwock Kim: "The Couple Next Door," "Hanji: Notes for a Paper-Maker," "Monologue for an Onion," and "Montage with Neon . . ." from *Notes from the Divided Country* (Louisiana State University Press) by Sue Kwock Kim. © 2003 by Sue Kwock Kim. Reprinted by permission of Louisiana State University Press. "The Couple Next Door" first appeared in the *Michigan Quarterly Review*. "Hanji" first appeared in *The Nation*. "Monologue for an Onion" first appeared in the *Paris Review*. "Montage with Neon . . ." first appeared in *PN Review*.

Li-Young Lee: "Persimmons" from *The Rose* (BOA Editions), by Li-Young Lee. © 1986 by Li-Young Lee. Reprinted by permission BOA Editions.

Timothy Liu: "Coup de Grâce," "An Evening Train," "The Assignation," "Winter," and "Monologue with the Void" from *Hard Evidence* (Talisman House Publishing) by Timothy Liu. © 2001 by Timothy Liu. Reprinted by permission of the author. "An Evening Train" first appeared in *Boulevard*. Reprinted by permission of the author. "The Assignation" first appeared in *Tin House*. Reprinted by permission of the author.

Warren Liu: "Li Po Declines" first appeared in *ZYZZYVA*. Reprinted by permission of the author. "El Niño" first appeared in *Interlope*. Reprinted by permission of the author and the editor of *Interlope*. "Be You Ever So Lonesome" reprinted by permission of the author.

Mông-Lan: "Ravine," "Field," "Letters," and "Emerald World" from *Song of the Cicadas* (University of Massachusetts Press) by Mông-Lan. © 2001 by Mông-Lan. Reprinted by permission of the author and the University of Massachusetts Press. "Ravine" and "Field" first appeared in the *Kenyon Review*. Reprinted by permission of the author. "Letters" first appeared in *Five Fingers Review*. Reprinted by permission of the author. "Emerald World" first appeared in *Berkeley Poetry Review*. Reprinted by permission of the author. "Overhearing Water" first appeared in *CutBank*. Reprinted by permission of the author.

Aimee Nezhukumatathil: "A Date with a Cherry Farmer," "Red Ghazal," "Fishbone," "Mouth Stories," and "What I Learned from the Incredible Hulk" from

Miracle Fruit (Tupelo Press) by Aimee Nezhukumatathil. © 2003 by Aimee Nezhukumatathil. "Mouth Stories" was the winner of the 1999 *Atlantic Monthly*'s Emerging Writer Competition and first appeared in *Fishbone* (Snail's Pace Press). © 2000 by Aimee Nezhukumatathil. "A Date with a Cherry Farmer" first appeared in *Poetry Northwest*. "Fishbone" first appeared in *Babaylan: An Anthology of Filipina and Filipina American Writers* (Aunt Lute Books). "Red Ghazal" first appeared in *The MacGuffin*. "What I Learned from the Incredible Hulk" first appeared in *Mid-American Review*. All poems reprinted by permission of the author.

Rick Noguchi: "The Shirt His Father Wore That Day Was Wrinkled, Slightly," "From Rooftops, Kenji Takezo Throws Himself," and "The Ocean Inside Him" from *The Ocean Inside Kenji Takezo* (University of Pittsburgh Press) by Rick Noguchi. © 1996. Reprinted by permission of the author and the University of Pittsburgh Press. "With Her at All Times . . ." and "A Man Made Himself a Marionette" reprinted by permission of the author.

Jon Pineda: "Shelter" appeared in *Literary Review*. Reprinted by permission of the author. "This Poetry" appeared in *64 Magazine*. Reprinted by permission of the author. "Losing a Memory" appeared in *Hayden's Ferry Review*. Reprinted by permission of the author. "Birthmark" and "Translation" reprinted by permission of the author.

Srikanth Reddy: "Burial Practice" appeared in *Volt*. Reprinted by permission of the author. "Hotel Lullaby" appeared in *Verse*. Reprinted by permission of the author. "Circle (VI)" appeared in *Lit*. Reprinted by permission of the author. "Circle (I)" and "Palinode" reprinted by permission of the author.

Paisley Rekdal: "Stupid," "Anniversary Song," "25% Pressure," and "Death and the Maiden" from *Six Girls without Pants* (Eastern Washington University Press) by Paisley Rekdal. © 2002 by Paisley Rekdal. Reprinted by permission of the author and Eastern Washington University Press. "Stupid" first appeared in *Poetry Northwest*. Reprinted by permission of the author. "Anniversary Song" first appeared in *River City*. Reprinted by permission of the author. "25% Pressure" first appeared in *Crazyhorse*. Reprinted by permission of the author.

Lee Ann Roripaugh: "Transplanting," "Hope," and "Dream Carp" reprinted by permission of the author.

Brenda Shaughnessy: "Rise," "Your One Good Dress," "Postfeminism," "Panopticon," and "Interior with Sudden Joy" from *Interior with Sudden Joy* (Farrar, Straus, and Giroux) by Brenda Shaughnessy. © 1999 by Brenda Shaughnessy. Reprinted by permission of the author and Farrar, Straus, and Giroux. "Interior with Sudden Joy" first appeared in the *Paris Review*. Reprinted by permission of the author.

Adrienne Su: "The English Canon," "Female Infanticide: A Guide for Mothers," "Savannah Crabs," and "Wedding Gifts" from *Middle Kingdom* (Alice James Books) by Adrienne Su. © 1997 by Adrienne Su. Reprinted by permission of Alice James Books. "The English Canon" and "Female Infanticide: A Guide for Mothers" first appeared in *New Letters*. Reprinted by permission of the author. "Wedding Gifts" first appeared in the *Indiana Review*. Reprinted by permission of the author. "Savannah Crabs" first appeared in *Clockwatch Review*. Reprinted by permission of the author.

Pimone Triplett: "Bird of Paradise . . . ," "Comings and Goings," "To My Cousin in Bangkok, Age 16," "Stillborn," and "Winter Swim" from *Ruining the Picture* (Northwestern University Press/TriQuarterly Press) by Pimone Triplett. © 1998 by Pimone Triplett. Reprinted by permission of the author and TriQuarterly Press. "Bird of Paradise . . ." and "To My Cousin in Bangkok, Age 16" first appeared in the *New England Review*. Reprinted by permission of the author.

Monica Youn: "25th & Dolores," "Korean Martyrs," "Flatlanders," "Décor," and "Venice, Unaccompanied" from *Barter* (Graywolf Press) by Monica Youn. © 2003 by Monica Youn. Reprinted by permission of Graywolf Press. "25th and Dolores" and "Korean Martyrs" appeared in the *New England Review*. "Flatlanders" appeared in *Chelsea*. Reprinted by permission of the author.

C. Dale Young: "The Philosopher in Florida," "*Broughtonia*," and "Exile" from *The Day underneath the Day* (Northwestern University Press/TriQuarterly Press) by C. Dale Young. © 2001 by C. Dale Young. Reprinted by permission of the author and TriQuarterly Press. "The Philosopher in Florida" first appeared in *Gulf Coast*. Reprinted by permission of the author. "*Broughtonia*" first appeared in *Ploughshares*. Reprinted by permission of the author. "Exile" first appeared in *Western Humanities Review*. Reprinted by permission of the author. "Moonlight Cocktail" appeared in *Southwest Review*. Reprinted by permission of the author. "Invective" appeared in *Chelsea*. Reprinted by permission of the author.

Contributors

Lisa Asagi is the author of *Physics* (2001) and *Twelve Scenes from 12 A.M.* (2001), published by Tinfish Press. Her work has appeared in journals, anthologies, magazines, and as art/objects. Her other work includes interdisciplinary performance as well as collaborative writing, visual art, and Web-based projects. Born and raised in Hawaii, she is currently based in San Francisco and Honolulu.

Rick Barot is currently the Jenny McKean Moore Visiting Writer at George Washington University. He was born in the Philippines and grew up in the San Francisco Bay Area. He was educated at Wesleyan University, the Writers' Workshop at the University of Iowa, and Stanford, where he was a Wallace E. Stegner Fellow. In 2001 he received a fellowship from the National Endowment for the Arts. His first book, *The Darker Fall,* was published in 2002 by Sarabande Books.

Nick Carbó is the author of two books of poetry published by Tia Chucha Press: *El Grupo McDonald's* (1995) and *Secret Asian Man* (1995). He is the editor of the groundbreaking anthology of Filipino and Filipino American poetry, *Returning a Borrowed Tongue* (Coffee House Press, 1996), and the coeditor with Eileen Tabios of *Babaylan: An Anthology of Filipina and Filipina American Writers* (Aunt Lute Books, 2000). Among his awards are fellowships in poetry from the National Endowment for the Arts and the New York Foundation for the Arts. He lives in Miami, Florida, with his wife, the poet Denise Duhamel.

Jennifer Chang was educated at the University of Chicago and the University of Virginia, where she received her MFA as a Henry Hoyns Fellow. Her works has appeared in *Beloit Poetry Journal, CROWD, Hayden's Ferry Review,* the *Indiana Review, Prairie Schooner, Seneca Review,* and other journals. She has received fellowships and grants from the Barbara Deming Memorial Fund, the Djerassi Resident Artists Program, Geraldine R. Dodge Foundation, and the MacDowell Colony. Born and raised in New Jersey, she lives in Brooklyn with her husband, the poet Aaron Baker.

Tina Chang's poems have appeared in *Ploughshares, Quarterly West,* the *Missouri Review,* the *Indiana Review, Sonora Review,* and *Cream City Review,* among others. Her poems have been anthologized in *Identity Lessons* (Penguin Putnam, 1999), *Poetry Nation* (Vehicle Press, 1998), and *Asian American Literature* (McGraw-Hill, 2001). She has received awards from the Academy of American Poets, *Poets & Writers,* the Ludwig Vogelstein Foundation, the Van Lier Foundation, the Barbara Deming Memorial Fund, and she has held writing fellowships from Villa Montalvo, Fundacion Valparaiso, Vermont Studio Center, and the MacDowell Colony. She is the recipient of a 2003 poetry grant from the New York Foundation for the Arts. Her first collection of poetry, *Half-Lit Houses,* is forthcoming from Four Way Books in Spring 2004.

Victoria M. Chang won the Crab Orchard Review Award Series in Poetry and her first book of poetry will be published in 2005 by the Southern Illinois University Press. Her poems have appeared in journals such as *The Nation,* the *North American Review,* the *New England Review, DoubleTake,* the *Massachusetts Review, Michigan Quarterly Review, Threepenny Review,* and *Pleiades.* She was educated at the University of Michigan, Harvard, and Stanford, and she is currently attending Warren Wilson's MFA program on a Holden Minority Scholarship. She has received a Bread Loaf Scholarship, a Taylor Fellowship, and a Hopwood Award. She resides in Los Angeles and San Diego.

Marilyn Chin is the author of *The Phoenix Gone, the Terrace Empty* (PEN Josephine Miles Award, 1994) and *Dwarf Bamboo* (nominated for the Bay Area Book Reviewer's Award in 1987). Both books have become Asian American classics and are taught in numerous classrooms nationally. She also coedited *Dissident Song,* a contemporary Asian American anthology (Quarry West, 1991), and cotranslated *The Selected Poems of Ai Qing* (Indiana University Press, 1985). Recently, her poetry has appeared in *Ms.,* the *Kenyon Review,* the *Iowa Review, Parnassus,* and *ZYZZYVA,* among others. Her poetry is widely anthologized, most recently in *The Open Boat* (Anchor, 1993) and the *Norton Introduction to Poetry* (2003). She is a recipient of a Stegner Fellowship from Stanford, two National Endowment for the Arts Fellowships, and the Mary Roberts Rinehart Award in creative writing. She has received residencies at Yaddo, the MacDowell Colony, the Djerassi Foundation, the Virginia Center for the Creative Arts, Centrum, and Villa Montalvo. She has recited her work all over the country. She was the guest poet at the Library of Congress, introduced by the Poet Laureate Rita Dove. She has read at Harvard, Yale, the University of Chicago, the Geraldine R. Dodge Festival, and the University of California at Berkeley. Born in Hong Kong and raised in Portland, Oregon, she considers the Pacific Rim her home and San Diego her most recent place of exile.

Oliver de la Paz was born in Manila, Philippines, and raised in Ontario, Oregon. He received his MFA from Arizona State University and has taught creative writing at Arizona State University and Gettysburg College. He is currently an assistant professor at Utica College. His work has appeared in journals such as *Quarterly West, North American Review, Third Coast,* the *Asian Pacific American Journal,* and in the anthology *Tilting the Continent: Southeast Asian American Literature.* His book of prose and verse, *Names above Houses,* was published by Southern Illinois University Press in 2001.

Marisa de los Santos was born in Baltimore, Maryland, and raised in northern Virginia. She received an MFA from Sarah Lawrence College and a Ph.D. from the University of Houston. Her poems have appeared in numerous journals, including *Poetry,* the *Southwest Review,* and *Prairie Schooner,* and her collection *From the Bones Out* was published by the University of South Carolina Press in 2000. She teaches at the University of Delaware and lives in Philadelphia with her husband, David Teague, and their children, Charles and Annabel.

Brian Komei Dempster completed his MFA in creative writing at the University of Michigan and was a recipient of a Creative Artist Grant from the Arts Foundation of Michigan and the Michigan Council for Arts and Cultural Affairs. He has also been awarded residency fellowships to the Ragdale Foundation, Ucross Foundation, Vermont Studio Center, and Villa Montalvo. His poems have appeared in the *Asian Pacific American Journal, Crab Orchard Review, Fourteen Hills, Green Mountains Review, Gulf Coast, Ploughshares, Post Road, Prairie Schooner,* and *Quarterly West.* He is the editor of *From Our Side of the Fence: Growing Up in America's Concentration Camps* (Kearny Street Workshop, 2001).

Linh Dinh is the author of a collection of stories, *Fake House* (Seven Stories Press, 2000), and several collections of poetry, including *All Around What Empties Out* (Tinfish Press, 2003). His poems are anthologized in *Best American Poetry 2000* and *Great American Prose Poems from Poe to the Present,* and he is also the editor of the anthologies *Night, Again: Contemporary Fiction from Vietnam* (Seven Stories Press, 1996) and *Three Vietnamese Poets* (Tinfish Press, 2001). He is living in Certaldo, Italy, as a guest of the International Parliament of Writers.

Monica Ferrell, a 2002–4 Wallace Stegner Fellow at Stanford University, has been a 2001 "Discovery"/The Nation winner and 2002 grant recipient of the MacDowell Colony and Van Lier Fellow of the Asian American Writers' Workshop. Her poems have appeared in *The Nation,* the *Paris Review,* the *Boston Review, Fence, Tin House,* the *New England Review,* and other journals. She holds a B.A. from Harvard College and an MFA from Columbia University.

Cathy Park Hong grew up in Los Angeles and currently lives in Brooklyn. She has an MFA from the Iowa Writers' Workshop. She has worked for the *Village Voice* and *The Source* magazine, has won the Van Lier Fellowship for Poetry, the New York Foundation for the Arts Fellowship, and her work is included in the 2000 Pushcart Prize collection. Her collection of poems, *Translating Mo'um,* was published in 2004. She is currently working on her second manuscript, *Dance Dance Revolution.*

Antonio Jocson received his MFA from the University of Iowa Writers' Workshop. He has published nine books for children and three sailing guides. His poems have appeared in various anthologies and journals such as *Ploughshares, Crab Orchard Review, Spoon River Quarterly,* and *Nimrod.* He lives in Houston, Texas, where he is an assistant professor of English at Prairie View A&M University, part of the Texas A&M system.

Vandana Khanna was born in New Delhi, India, and has lived most of her life in the United States. She received her MFA from Indiana University, where she was a recipient of the Yellen Fellowship in poetry. Her first book of poetry, *Train to Agra,* won the 2000 Crab Orchard Review First Book Prize and was published in 2001 by Southern Illinois University Press. Her poems have appeared in *Callaloo, Crazyhorse,* and *Hayden's Ferry Review,* among others.

Suji Kwock Kim was educated at Yale College, the Iowa Writers' Workshop, and Stanford University. Her first book, *Notes from the Divided Country,* was selected by Yusef Komunyakaa as the winner of the 2002 Walt Whitman Award of the Academy of American Poets. Her poems have appeared in *The Nation,* the *New Republic,* the *Paris Review, Poetry,* the *Yale Review, DoubleTake, Threepenny Review, Tin House,* the *New England Review, Salmagundi,* the *Southwest Review, Ploughshares,* the *Harvard Review, Columbia,* the *Michigan Quarterly Review,* and other journals and anthologies. She is the recipient of National Endowment for the Arts, Fulbright, Stegner, and Fine Arts Work Center in Provincetown Fellowships as well as the "Discovery"/The Nation Award and grants from the New York Foundation for the Arts, the California Arts Council, and the Washington State Artist Trust. *Private Property,* a multimedia play she cowrote, was produced at the Edinburgh Festival Fringe. She is an assistant professor of English at Drew University.

Mông-Lan, a visual artist and writer, came to the United States as a child after the political upheaval of Saigon, Vietnam, in 1975. Her first book of poems, *Song of the Cicadas,* won the Juniper Prize and was published by the University of Massachusetts Press in 2001. It won the Great Lakes Colleges Association's Prize for New Writers and was a finalist for the Poetry Society of America's Norma Faber First Book Award. Her work has been included in the *Pushcart Prize Anthology XXIV,* the *Best American Poetry of 2002,* and in many journals such as the *Kenyon Review,* the *Colorado Review,* the *Iowa Review,* and *New American Writing.* She received the Dean's MFA Fellowship from the University of Arizona, a Stegner Fellowship from Stanford University, and a Fulbright Grant to Vietnam.

Timothy Liu is the author of four books of poems, most recently *Hard Evidence* (Talisman House, 2001). Two new books are forthcoming: *Of Thee I Sing* (University of Georgia Press, 2004) and *E Pluribus Unum a.k.a. Kamikaze Pilots in Paradise* (Southern Illinois University Press, 2005). An associate professor at William Paterson University, Liu lives in Hoboken, N.J.

Warren Liu was born and raised in Buffalo, New York. He received his MFA in creative writing from the University of Iowa. His poems have appeared in *Interlope, Faucheuse,* the *Chicago Review, ZYZZYVA, Chain,* and other journals.

He is currently a graduate student at the University of California at Berkeley, where he is working on a dissertation about contemporary Asian American poetry.

Aimee Nezhukumatathil was born in Chicago to a Filipina mother and an East Indian father in 1974. She received her MFA from Ohio State University and was a fellow at the Wisconsin Institute for Creative Writing at the University of Wisconsin–Madison. Her chapbook, *Fishbone,* won the Snail's Pace Press Prize, and her first full-length collection, *Miracle Fruit* (Tupelo Press, 2003), won the Tupelo Press First Book Prize. Awards for her writing include the Boatwright Prize from *Shenandoah,* the Richard Hugo Award from *Poetry Northwest,* and an AWP Intro Award. Her poems have appeared in *Beloit Poetry Journal, Prairie Schooner, Slate, Shenandoah,* the *Southern Review,* and *Virginia Quarterly Review.* She lives in the heart of cherry and berry country in western New York and is an assistant professor of English at the State University of New York at Fredonia.

Rick Noguchi received his MFA in creative writing from Arizona State University. His first book of poems, *The Ocean Inside Kenji Takezo,* received the Associated Writing Programs Award in Poetry in 1995 and was published by the University of Pittsburgh Press. Other publications include *The Wave He Caught,* which won the Pearl Editions Prize in 1994, and most recently a children's book, *Flowers from Mariko* (Lee and Low Books, 2001), which he cowrote with his wife, Deneen Jenks. His poems have appeared in numerous anthologies. He currently serves as the program manager of the UCLA Extension Writers' Program.

Jon Pineda is a graduate of James Madison University and has studied in the MFA program in creative writing at Virginia Commonwealth University. His first poetry collection, *Birthmark,* was chosen by Ralph Burns as the winner of the 2003 Crab Orchard Award Series Open Competition and will be published by Southern Illinois University Press in 2004.

Srikanth Reddy is currently the poet-in-residence at the University of Chicago. He was educated at Harvard and the University of Iowa. His work has appeared in various literary journals, including *American Poetry Review, Grand Street, Fence,* and the *Harvard Review.* His first collection of poetry, *Facts for Visitors,* is forthcoming in Spring 2004 from the University of California Press.

Paisley Rekdal is the author of a book of essays, *The Night My Mother Met Bruce Lee* (Pantheon, 2000), and two books of poetry, *A Crash of Rhinos* (University of Georgia Press, 2000) and *Six Girls without Pants* (Eastern Washington University Press, 2002). She is the recipient of a Village Voice Writers on the Verge Award, the University of Georgia Press's Contemporary Poetry Series Award, a Fulbright Fellowship, an NEA Fellowship, the Lawrence Goldstein Poetry Award, and the Wyoming Arts Council Literary Fellowship. Her work has appeared on *National Public Radio* and in the *New York Times Sunday Magazine, Nerve,* the *Michigan Quarterly Review,* the *Denver Quarterly, Black Warrior Review, Ploughshares,* the *Indiana Review,* and *Poetry Northwest,* among others.

Lee Ann Roripaugh's first volume of poetry, *Beyond Heart Mountain* (Penguin Books, 1999), was a 1998 winner of the National Poetry Series and was selected as a finalist for the 2000 Asian American Literary Awards. Her second volume of poetry, *Year of the Snake,* was the second-prize winner of the Crab Orchard Review Poetry Series Prize and is forthcoming from Southern Illinois University Press in 2004. A 2003 recipient of a Bush Artist Fellowship, her poetry and fiction have appeared or are forthcoming in journals such as *Ploughshares, Shenandoah,* the *Michigan Quarterly Review, Grand Street, Parnassus,* the *New England Review, North American Review,* and *Crab Orchard Review,* among others. She is currently an assistant professor of English at the University of South Dakota, where she is associate editor of the *South Dakota Review.*

Brenda Shaughnessy was born in Okinawa, Japan, in 1970 and grew up in Southern California. She received her B.A. in literature and women's studies at the University of California at Santa Cruz, and she earned an MFA at Columbia University's Writing Division. She is the author of *Interior with Sudden Joy* (Farrar, Straus, and Giroux, 1999), which was nominated for a Lambda Literary Award, and she was a finalist for the PEN/Joyce Osterweil Award and the Poetry Society of America's Norma Farber First Book Award. Her other honors include an Emerging Artist's Award from the Greenwall Foundation and New York University's Institute for Advanced Study, a Creative Artist's Fellowship from the Japan/U.S. Friendship Commission, and a Bunting Fellowship. Her poems have appeared in such publications as *Best American Poetry 2000,* the *Boston Review, Chelsea, Conjunctions,* the *Paris Review,* and the *Yale Review.* She lives in New York City.

Adrienne Su, author of *Middle Kingdom* (Alice James, 1997), is poet-in-residence at Dickinson College in Carlisle, Pennsylvania. Her poems have been anthologized in *The New American Poets, American Poetry: The Next Generation, Ravishing Disunities, The Pushcart Prize,* and others, and her prose has appeared in *Girls* and *The NuyorAsian Anthology.* She has received fellowships from the Fine Arts Work Center in Provincetown and Dartmouth College, and she was the 2003 poet-in-residence at the Frost Place in Franconia, New Hampshire.

Pimone Triplett is the author of *Ruining the Picture* (TriQuarterly Press, 1998). Her poems have appeared or are forthcoming in the *Yale Review, Agni,* the *New England Review,* the *Paris Review, Pequod, Poetry, Triquarterly,* and many other journals. Anthologies that have featured her work include *The New American Poets: A Bread Loaf Anthology* and *American Poetry: The Next Generation.*

She has a B.A. from Sarah Lawrence and an MFA from the Iowa Writers' Workshop. She is a professor of creative writing at the University of Oregon.

Monica Youn's poems have appeared in *Agni, American Letters & Commentary,* the *Denver Quarterly, Fence, LIT, Poetry Review,* and many other journals. Her first book, *Barter,* will be published by Graywolf Press in 2004. She currently practices intellectual property law in Manhattan.

C. Dale Young practices medicine (radiation oncology) in the San Francisco Bay Area and serves as the poetry editor of the *New England Review.* He is the author of *The Day underneath the Day* (TriQuarterly Books, 2001), which was a finalist for the 2002 Norma Farber Award. A previous recipient of the Grolier Prize, the Tennessee Williams Scholarship in Poetry from the Sewanee Writers' Conference, and the Stanley P. Young Fellowship in Poetry from the Bread Loaf Writers' Conference, his poems have appeared in many anthologies and magazines, including *The Best American Poetry.* He lives in San Francisco.

Index of Titles

Illinois Poetry Series

Laurence Lieberman, Editor

History Is Your Own Heartbeat
Michael S. Harper (1971)

The Foreclosure
Richard Emil Braun (1972)

The Scrawny Sonnets and Other
Narratives
Robert Bagg (1973)

The Creation Frame
Phyllis Thompson (1973)

To All Appearances: Poems New and
Selected
Josephine Miles (1974)

The Black Hawk Songs
Michael Borich (1975)

Nightmare Begins Responsibility
Michael S. Harper (1975)

The Wichita Poems
Michael Van Walleghen (1975)

Images of Kin: New and Selected
Poems
Michael S. Harper (1977)

Poems of the Two Worlds
Frederick Morgan (1977)

Cumberland Station
Dave Smith (1977)

Tracking
Virginia R. Terris (1977)

Riversongs
Michael Anania (1978)

On Earth as It Is
Dan Masterson (1978)

Coming to Terms
Josephine Miles (1979)

Death Mother and Other Poems
Frederick Morgan (1979)

Goshawk, Antelope
Dave Smith (1979)

Local Men
James Whitehead (1979)

Searching the Drowned Man
Sydney Lea (1980)

With Akhmatova at the Black Gates
Stephen Berg (1981)

Dream Flights
Dave Smith (1981)

More Trouble with the Obvious
Michael Van Walleghen (1981)

The American Book of the Dead
Jim Barnes (1982)

The Floating Candles
Sydney Lea (1982)

Northbook
Frederick Morgan (1982)

Collected Poems, 1930–83
Josephine Miles (1983; reissue, 1999)

The River Painter
Emily Grosholz (1984)

Healing Song for the Inner Ear
Michael S. Harper (1984)

The Passion of the Right-Angled Man
T. R. Hummer (1984)

Dear John, Dear Coltrane
Michael S. Harper (1985)

Poems from the Sangamon
John Knoepfle (1985)

In It
Stephen Berg (1986)

The Ghosts of Who We Were
Phyllis Thompson (1986)

Moon in a Mason Jar
Robert Wrigley (1986)

Lower-Class Heresy
T. R. Hummer (1987)

Poems: New and Selected
Frederick Morgan (1987)

Furnace Harbor: A Rhapsody of the
North Country
Philip D. Church (1988)

Bad Girl, with Hawk
Nance Van Winckel (1988)

Blue Tango
Michael Van Walleghen (1989)

Eden
Dennis Schmitz (1989)

Waiting for Poppa at the Smithtown
Diner
Peter Serchuk (1990)

Great Blue
Brendan Galvin (1990)

What My Father Believed
Robert Wrigley (1991)

Something Grazes Our Hair
S. J. Marks (1991)

Walking the Blind Dog
G. E. Murray (1992)

The Sawdust War
Jim Barnes (1992)

The God of Indeterminacy
Sandra McPherson (1993)

Off-Season at the Edge of the World
Debora Greger (1994)

Counting the Black Angels
Len Roberts (1994)

Oblivion
Stephen Berg (1995)

To Us, All Flowers Are Roses
Lorna Goodison (1995)

Honorable Amendments
Michael S. Harper (1995)

Points of Departure
Miller Williams (1995)

Dance Script with Electric Ballerina
Alice Fulton (reissue, 1996)

To the Bone: New and Selected Poems
Sydney Lea (1996)

Floating on Solitude
Dave Smith (3-volume reissue, 1996)

Bruised Paradise
Kevin Stein (1996)

Walt Whitman Bathing
David Wagoner (1996)

Rough Cut
Thomas Swiss (1997)

Paris
Jim Barnes (1997)

The Ways We Touch
Miller Williams (1997)

The Rooster Mask
Henry Hart (1998)

The Trouble-Making Finch
Len Roberts (1998)

Grazing
Ira Sadoff (1998)

Turn Thanks
Lorna Goodison (1999)

Traveling Light:
Collected and New Poems
David Wagoner (1999)

Some Jazz a While:
Collected Poems
Miller Williams (1999)

The Iron City
John Bensko (2000)

Songlines in Michaeltree: New and
Collected Poems
Michael S. Harper (2000)

Pursuit of a Wound
Sydney Lea (2000)

The Pebble: Old and New Poems
Mairi MacInnes (2000)

Chance Ransom
Kevin Stein (2000)

House of Poured-Out Waters
Jane Mead (2001)

The Silent Singer: New and Selected
Poems
Len Roberts (2001)

The Salt Hour
J. P. White (2001)

Guide to the Blue Tongue
Virgil Suárez (2002)

The House of Song
David Wagoner (2002)

X =
Stephen Berg (2002)

Arts of a Cold Sun
G. E. Murray (2003)

Barter
Ira Sadoff (2003)

The Hollow Log Lounge
R. T. Smith (2003)

National Poetry Series

Eroding Witness
Nathaniel Mackey (1985)
Selected by Michael S. Harper

Palladium
Alice Fulton (1986)
Selected by Mark Strand

Cities in Motion
Sylvia Moss (1987)
Selected by Derek Walcott

The Hand of God and a Few
Bright Flowers
William Olsen (1988)
Selected by David Wagoner

The Great Bird of Love
Paul Zimmer (1989)
Selected by William Stafford

Stubborn
Roland Flint (1990)
Selected by Dave Smith

The Surface
Laura Mullen (1991)
Selected by C. K. Williams

The Dig
Lynn Emanuel (1992)
Selected by Gerald Stern

My Alexandria
Mark Doty (1993)
Selected by Philip Levine

The High Road to Taos
Martin Edmunds (1994)
Selected by Donald Hall

Theater of Animals
Samn Stockwell (1995)
Selected by Louise Glück

The Broken World
Marcus Cafagña (1996)
Selected by Yusef Komunyakaa

Nine Skies
A. V. Christie (1997)
Selected by Sandra McPherson

Lost Wax
Heather Ramsdell (1998)
Selected by James Tate

So Often the Pitcher Goes to Water
until It Breaks
Rigoberto González (1999)
Selected by Ai

Renunciation
Corey Marks (2000)
Selected by Philip Levine

Manderley
Rebecca Wolff (2001)
Selected by Robert Pinsky

Theory of Devolution
David Groff (2002)
Selected by Mark Doty

Rhythm and Booze
Julie Kane (2003)
Selected by Maxine Kumin

Other Poetry Volumes

Local Men and *Domains*
James Whitehead (1987)

Her Soul beneath the Bone: Women's
Poetry on Breast Cancer
Edited by Leatrice Lifshitz (1988)

Days from a Dream Almanac
Dennis Tedlock (1990)

Working Classics: Poems on Industrial
Life
*Edited by Peter Oresick and Nicholas
Coles* (1990)

Hummers, Knucklers, and Slow
Curves: Contemporary Baseball Poems
Edited by Don Johnson (1991)

The Double Reckoning of Christopher
Columbus
Barbara Helfgott Hyett (1992)

Selected Poems
Jean Garrigue (1992)

New and Selected Poems, 1962–92
Laurence Lieberman (1993)

The Dig and *Hotel Fiesta*
Lynn Emanuel (1994)

For a Living: The Poetry of Work
*Edited by Nicholas Coles and Peter
Oresick* (1995)

The Tracks We Leave: Poems on
Endangered Wildlife of North America
Barbara Helfgott Hyett (1996)

Peasants Wake for Fellini's *Casanova*
and Other Poems
*Andrea Zanzotto; edited and translated
by John P. Welle and Ruth Feldman;
drawings by Federico Fellini and
Augusto Murer* (1997)

Moon in a Mason Jar and *What My
Father Believed*
Robert Wrigley (1997)

The Wild Card: Selected Poems, Early
and Late
*Karl Shapiro; edited by Stanley Kunitz
and David Ignatow* (1998)

Turtle, Swan and *Bethlehem in Broad
Daylight*
Mark Doty (2000)

Illinois Voices: An Anthology of
Twentieth-Century Poetry
Edited by Kevin Stein and G. E. Murray
(2001)

On a Wing of the Sun
Jim Barnes (3-volume reissue, 2001)

Poems
William Carlos Williams; introduction by Virginia M. Wright-Peterson (2002)

Creole Echoes: The Francophone Poetry of Nineteenth-Century Louisiana
Translated by Norman R. Shapiro; introduction and notes by M. Lynn Weiss (2003)

Poetry from *Sojourner:* A Feminist Anthology
Edited by Ruth Lepson with Lynne Yamaguchi; introduction by Mary Loeffelholz (2003)

Asian American Poetry: The Next Generation
Edited by Victoria M. Chang; foreword by Marilyn Chin (2004)

The Univers
is a foundin
Association

———————

Composed i
with Meta d
for the Univ
Designed by
Manufactured by Thomson-Shore, Inc.

University of Illinois Press
1325 South Oak Street   Champaign, IL 61820-6903
www.press.uillinois.edu